China's Overseas Investment in the Belt and Road Era

Globalization Monitor

Email: info@globalmon.org.hk

Published in Aug 2021

All rights reserved.

The contents of this report may be reproduced in non-profit publication. Credit is requested.

www.globalmon.org.hk

Acknowledgement

Globalization Monitor would like to thank Forum Arbeitswelten for its support in the research on Part 8, Chinese Investment in Germany.

Source of the cover picture: shorturl.at/irCX2

CONTENTS

Part 1: China's Overseas Investment Strategies from 'Going Global' to the Belt and Road Initiative — p.6-21

Part 2: Spotlight on Belt and Road Routes — p.22-29

Part 3: Financing China's Investments Overseas — p.30-38

Part 4: Hong Kong's role in Chinese Overseas Investment — p.39-47

Part 5: Strategic Companies and Overseas Investment: COSCO Shipping, CCCC and the Sinopec Group — p.48-66

Part 6: China in Africa — p.67-79

Part 7: China's Investments in Asia — p.83-95

Part 8: Chinese Investment in Germany — p.96-116

Part 9: Where does it lead? Challenges for Chinese Overseas Investment and the Belt and Road Initiative — p.117-128

References — p.129-145

Part 1: China's Overseas Investment Strategies from 'Going Global' to the Belt and Road Initiative

Let's work together to create a new Silk Road. Not a single thoroughfare like its namesake, but an international web and network of economic and transit connections. That means building more rail links, highways, energy infrastructure... It means upgrading the facilities at border crossings...removing the bureaucratic barriers and other impediments to the free flow of goods and people. It means casting aside the outdated trade policies that we all still are living with and adopting new rules for the 21st century[1].

The above quote is an excerpt from a speech given in Chennai, India, in 2011 by the then US Secretary of State Hillary Clinton entitled, 'Remarks on India and the United States: A Vision for the 21st Century'. Just two years later, however, it was President Xi Jinping of China, not the US and India, which was to draw on the historic legacy of the ancient Silk Road and announce plans to launch the Silk Road Economic Belt and the 21st Century Maritime Silk Road, later known collectively as the Belt and Road Initiative (BRI). Amongst the major official aims of Xi's initiative were the development of infrastructure networks, enhanced connectivity and unimpeded trade—from China across Asia, the Middle East, parts of Africa and into Europe.

The initiative, into which China planned to invest approximately $1.3 trillion by 2027 and possibly up to $8 trillion by its expected completion date of 2049, sounds ambitious. Nevertheless, given the country's own rapid domestic transformation and global rise, China's decision to implement such a grand initiative, which has the potential to impact on millions of lives around the globe, should not be taken lightly.

Source: shorturl.at/irCX2

From 'inviting in' to 'going out'

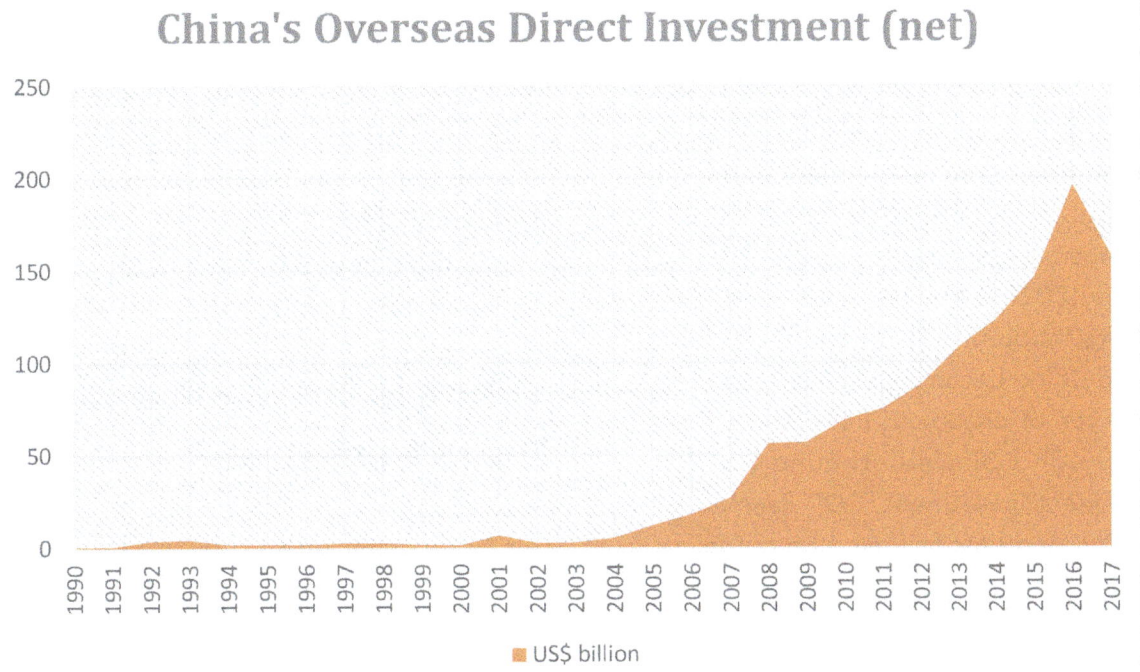

While the history of the ancient Silk Road dates back to the 2nd century BCE, the recent path to the BRI can be traced back to the economic changes that have occurred in China from the late 1970s. Indeed, since China first embarked on its reform and open policy in 1978, not only has its own economy undergone dramatic transformation, but there has also been drastic changes in the international division of labour and the global economy, in which China has come to play a pivotal role.

The greatest changes from a global perspective began from the 1990s, when China began to enter its second stage of reform and to more fully reintegrate into the global capitalist economy. This stage involved reliance on an export oriented or yinjinlai "inviting in" strategy, which led to huge amounts of FDI pouring into the country. The influxes of capital combined with the intensive exploitation of China's rural migrant labour force, turned China into the 'world's factory' and resulted in incredible economic growth rates, averaging 9.1% between March 1992 and December 2019[2].

"Inviting in" was not without challenges for China, however. Already in 1998, competition resulting from the decentralisation that accompanied market reform, and had ensued between different provinces and regions investing in the same industries, had resulted in significant overcapacity. Subsequently, the State Economic and Trade Committee released the Index of Over-Invested Products for Moving Abroad. Increasingly, moving overinvested productive capacity abroad also became seen as beneficial not only for turning idle capacity into revenue but also for earning more foreign currency.[3]

A year later, in the lead up to China's accession to the World Trade Organisation (WTO), a new stage in China's relationship with the global economy was fully signaled with the initiation of the zouchuqu "Going

Out" or "Going Global" strategy by the Chinese government. This strategy was designed specifically to promote overseas investment by Chinese companies. From the mid-2000s, onwards this strategy really took off and there has been a significant increase in outbound investment since then; both FDI and Foreign Portfolio Investment (FPI), as well as financial investment and international lending. In 2015 China's outbound FDI overtook its inbound FDI for the first time, and in 2016 China became the world's second largest source of outbound FDI for the first time. Although China's outbound FDI (or Overseas Direct Investment, ODI) seemed to peak in 2016 and was followed by a decline the following year (see chart below) when the Chinese government, seeking greater control, imposed some new restrictions, levels remain significantly higher than a decade earlier.

At the same time, and in part aided by overseas investments' facilitation of greater access to overseas markets, Chinese transnational corporations have also experienced a significant rise. While in 1995, China only had 2 TNCs listed in the Fortune 500, by 2019 the number had grown to 119[4], only two fewer than the US which had 121 listed that year. Significantly, of these Chinese companies included on the list in 2019, 80.2% were Chinese State-Owned Companies (SOEs)[5], reflecting how Chinese state capital is the lead beneficiary of the recent development agenda pursued so intentionally by the Chinese party-state.

With China's role in the global economy having grown significantly in recent decades, allowing for an expansion in the influence of the Chinese party-state and many Chinese companies (as well as their enrichment) it is perhaps unsurprising that this has resulted in yet further pursuit of expansion and additional emphasis being placed on China's overseas economic activities. The launching of China's One Belt, One Road (OBOR), later renamed the Belt and Road Initiative (BRI), in 2015 can be viewed as a symbolic new stage in this expansion. Dubbed "globalization 2.0", the scale of this initiative has the potential to impact on the lives of billions of people around the globe. Indeed, with a combined population of 4.4 billion, those living along the planned new Silk Road account for 63% of the world's population[6].

What is the Belt and Road Initiative?

The BRI was first proposed by Xi Jinping in his visits to Central Asia and Southeast Asia in 2013 and was then included in the Resolution of the Third Plenum of the 18th Central Committee of the CCP. China officially began to implement the project from 2015. Drawing on the legacy of the ancient Silk Road, the initiative comprises the Silk Road Economic Belt (made up of six economic corridors), aiming to link China and Europe through Central Asia and the Middle East, and the 21st Century Maritime Silk Road which links to Asia and the Pacific. According to a Chinese government document outlining its vision for the BRI, the 'Vision and Actions on jointly building Silk Road Economic Belt and 21st-Century Maritime Silk Road' (the Vision and Action Plan), the initiative will embrace, "the trend towards a multipolar world, economic globalization, cultural diversity and greater IT application, is designed to uphold the global free trade regime and the open world economy in the spirit of open regional cooperation"[7]. According to this document, the aim is to develop trade and infrastructure networks and the initiative has five official major goals for cooperation:

Policy coordination intergovernmental cooperation and coordination of economic development strategies and policies.

Facilities connectivity improvement of infrastructure and establishing an infrastructure network connecting all the sub-regions of Asia, and between Asia, Europe and Africa. Points of focus include key passageways and unconnected roads, port infrastructure, civil aviation cooperation and infrastructure, energy infrastructure and cross border optical cables.

Unimpeded trade removal of investment and trade barriers, creation of a "sound business environment", opening of free trade areas, increased customs cooperation and information exchange, assistance in law enforcement, development of e-commerce. This goal also includes increased cooperation in the areas of agriculture, forestry and fisheries; exploration and development of oil, coal, natural gas and other energy sources; emerging industries such as biotechnology; improvements of labour and distribution of industrial supply chains; ecological progress and tackling climate change.

Financial integration deeper financial cooperation and the building of a currency stability system, investment and financing system and credit information system in Asia. Financial integration also includes joint efforts to establish the AIIB and BRICS New Development Bank as well as supporting governments and financial institutions in BRI countries with good credit ratings to issue Renminbi bonds in China.

People to people bonds cultural and academic exchanges, media cooperation, tourism, communication between political parties and organisations in BRI countries and medical assistance.

Following China's launch of the BRI, many Chinese financial institutions were quick to pledge significant amounts of money to finance BRI projects (see part 3). At the same time, the potential investment that the BRI promised attracted the interest of many countries seeking financing to support their own goals and development agendas. According to official media, between 2014 and 2017 about 50 Chinese SOEs had participated in around 1,700 BRI projects[8]. By 2018, the Chinese Ministry of Commerce reported that the annual non-financial investment by Chinese enterprises in 56 BRI countries had grown to US$15.64 billion (up 8.9% year on year), while turnover of foreign contracted projects in 63 BRI countries along Belt and Road routes had reached US$89.33 billion[9]. In total, by September 2018, China had listed 84 countries as a part of the BRI, the majority having signed some sort of BRI cooperation agreement. As for the goals of greater financial integration, efforts to push forward with the AIIB in particular also got off to a promising start for China.

So far, the BRI has become most widely known for having involved significant investments and projects related to the construction of trade and infrastructure networks, ports, power stations, oil and gas pipelines, railway lines, roads, bridges, telecommunications and agriculture, as well as the development of coal, oil, gas, hydropower, nuclear, wind and solar power. It should be noted, however, that these projects include many cases where the projects were underway or planned long before the BRI was launched, but which have subsequently been brought under its umbrella. This includes flagship projects such as the China-Pakistan Economic Corridor (CPEC).

Indeed, some have even questioned whether the BRI is really something tangible or achievable. It is a very ambitious initiative and has encountered numerous challenges. Moreover, in terms of the number of genuinely new projects successfully implemented and amounts invested, it might be considered as off to a somewhat slow start. But as an exercise which promotes China through its claiming of a legacy and construction of a vision for a globalized world in which China plays a critical part, it might for now be considered a remarkable success. The BRI has remained a very serious discussion point, rivals have expressed concern and devised counter initiatives, and, despite the numerous criticisms of the project that will be discussed in following chapters, an increasing number of countries and international institutions have been expressing interest in and signing up to the BRI in various ways. In the medium to longer term, such a vision is threatened by poor and failed delivery, but for now the BRI is an initiative which is politically prioritized by China and needs attention and monitoring, so as to understand China's international economic and political strategies with a view to averting or limiting potential human and ecological harm. This report is therefore significantly weighted towards discussion of BRI countries and regions, although it recognizes that the expansion of Chinese overseas investment is of global importance and that future further discussion will be needed on impacts in other regions, especially Latin America and the US.

The aims and advantages of overseas investments for China

China has presented its BRI and overseas investments as a 'win-win' situation for both China and the receiving countries. While on the one hand, the initiative might set out to alleviate some of China's economic challenges, enrich its leaders and corporations and advance overseas political influence, investment has the potential to bring much needed infrastructure to less economically developed countries or provide much needed capital to struggling companies in the West. For developing countries, Chinese loans have also sometimes been viewed as an alternative to lending from Western financial institutions and the destructive strings that have sometimes accompanied them. China's vision for the BRI by contrast pledges to uphold the, "Five Principles of Peaceful Coexistence: mutual respect for each other's sovereignty and territorial integrity, mutual non-aggression, mutual non-interference in each other's internal affairs, equality and mutual benefit, and peaceful coexistence"[10]. In this context and assuming that this statement is true, BRI investment might be viewed as somewhat attractive to overseas governments. Nevertheless, Chinese investment has not always been so mutually beneficial or without interference as the Chinese government might like to present; some investments have had very adverse consequences in recipient countries and left them with significant debt (from which China may benefit). If the initiative is successful, China, on the other hand, stands to gain both politically and economically from the continued upgrading of its status on the global stage.

Indeed, there are several factors driving China's ambitions in expanding investment activities overseas. One of these factors has been the need for energy and raw materials to drive its rapid economic growth. Since the mid-1990s, China has relied heavily on oil imports and grown to become the world's second largest oil consumer, and in 2017 the world's largest importer– importing an average of 8 million barrels of crude oil per day.[11] In order to avoid more costly sourcing from overseas, China has sought to acquire overseas energy and raw material resources. [12]It is therefore unsurprising that the Vision and Action Plan for the BRI specifically identifies the development of energy resources such as coal oil and natural gas as an area of pursuit. It should also be pointed out that one of the major loan models employed by China has involved resource back loans, for instance to Russia (which has received the largest loans from China), as well as to countries in Latin America and sub-Saharan Africa. According to the Natural Resource Government Institute these two regions together are said to have taken out $152 billion in oil, mineral and metal backed loans from China since 2004[13]. Such loans often pose a significant debt risk to the countries concerned.

Another major long-term reason has been China's overcapacity production. This is a problem that has long plagued China, especially in industries such as steel, cement and aluminum, and was one of the initial impetuses for China's 'going global strategy' from the late 1990s/early 200s. The problem was only heightened following the 2008 economic crisis. Overseas investment in infrastructure and the potential enhanced connectivity associated with the BRI helps with facilitating the opening of new markets to Chinese products and services, another aim of Chinese overseas investment.

While the problem of overcapacity has been an important driving factor in the pursuit of expansion overseas, it has nevertheless been questioned whether the BRI really has the potential to absorb much of China's industrial overcapacity[14]. Markets along the BRI, for instance, are said to be too small to absorb meaningful proportions of China's excess production, while products such as cement, steel and plate glass are difficult to economically export in large volumes. The risk of debt default by countries that are most likely to accept large loans from China, such as Pakistan and Cambodia, also pose a risk to the long-term success of this aim[15].

It is not only developing countries where China stands to benefit. In developed countries, advanced manufacturing and technological capabilities have been an additional key motivating factor for Chinese investors. Acquiring knowledge and production expertise from countries such as Germany is in line with China's 'Made in China 2025' strategy, which aims at the upgrading of manufacturing capabilities so as to meet China's goal of becoming a leading industrial nation by 2049.

Another goal for China with the BRI accompanying investment is 'unimpeded trade'. According to the Vision and Action Plan, this involves improving trade liberalisation facilitation and eliminating investment barriers. Commitment has been made by BRI leaders to opposing all forms of protectionism. Indeed, along with investment, China has stated its intent to increase trade with Belt and Road countries. According to a speech by CDB Chairman, Hu Huaibang, in January 2018 to the Asian Financial Forum held in Hong Kong, between 2014 and 2016 China's trade volumes with BRI countries reached $3 trillion. Hu then estimated that China would invest another $150 billion in these countries in the next five years and would import products worth $2 trillion[16].

Additional financial incentives include greater international use of the RMB. At the same time, with Beijing's massive foreign exchange reserves (amounting to US$13 trillion in 2016), the interest rates of investing in overseas infrastructure projects can potentially offer a more attractive alternative to investing in low-yielding US treasury bonds[17].

The expansion of investments overseas is not only potentially economically beneficial to China, however; it has also been viewed as a way to advance geopolitical goals or political influence. Acquiring assets in strategic locations, for instance, is a key objective. Such assets are not only economically beneficial due to the increased connectivity they provide, some assets also allow the country to potentially assert itself in a more dominant manner in the region. The Gwadar port, which has been returned to Chinese control and is being expanded along with the creation of a free trade zone in connection to the creation of the China-Pakistan Economic Corridor (CPEC) is an important example. The port is strategic not only due to its potential to shorten and secure routes for transporting oil and gas from gulf countries to China, its location also acts as an alternative to circumvent potential threats to China's energy imports should they be interrupted due to actions by rivals or due to territorial disputes in the South China Sea[18].

The possibility of the provision of loans and investments has also been a way for China to win over allies or leave countries dependent on China's good favour. The promise of investment has coincided with changes in diplomatic relations whereby countries have ended ties with Taiwan so as to establish relations with China. Recent examples include the Soloman Islands, which ended diplomatic relations with Taiwan in September 2019 after China reportedly offered US$500 million[19]; El Salavdor, the Dominican Republic and Burkina Faso, which all switched relations in 2018; and Panama in 2017 to name just a few.

Finally, domestic concerns have been another motivating factor for China. The BRI is also intended to support the development and reform of all provinces and regions within China, with different provinces and regions intended to have different functions within the plan and many also passing their own development plans in relation to this. Security has been another related issue motivating aspects of the BRI. In particular concerns about Islamic fundamentalism have often been cited, while the importance of the region's energy reserves have been of great importance to the government. With Xinjiang province a particularly important province for the BRI, the initiative has, however, coincided with even greater extreme repression and human rights violations that are having devastating consequences for much of the Uighur population living in Xinjiang province.

The aims and advantages of overseas investments for China

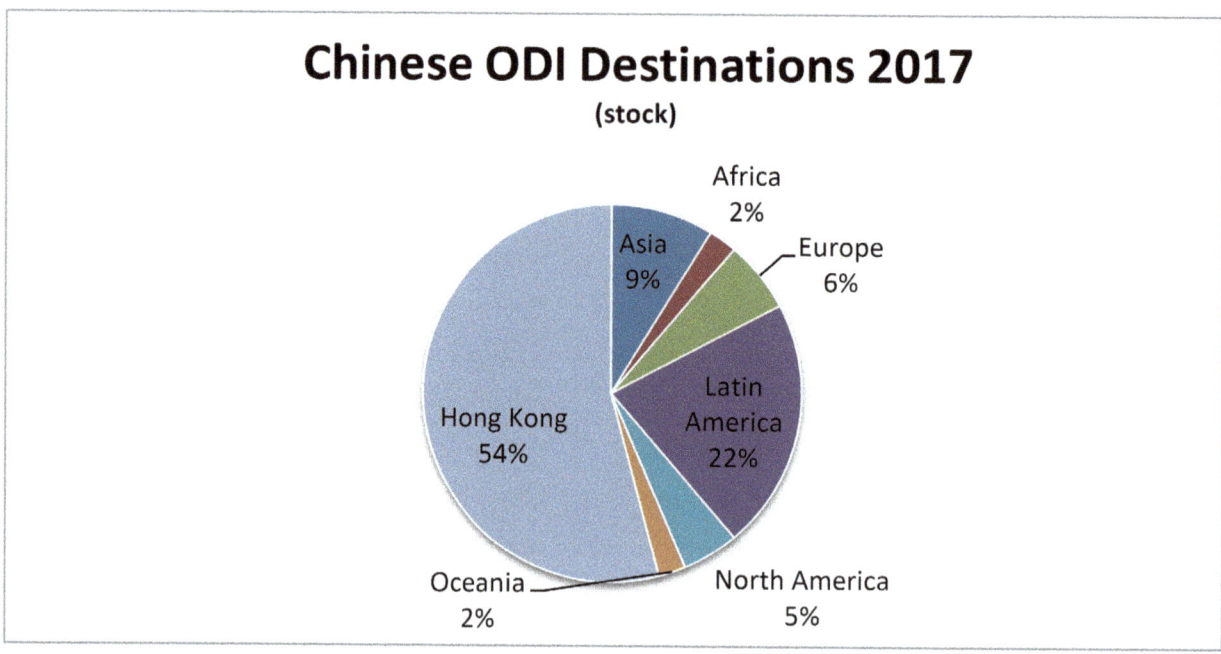

Data from China Statistical Yearbook 2018

Data from China Statistical Yearbooks

In the past, limited official statistics were made available on China's ODI. It was not until 2006 that the Chinese government released its first comprehensive report on ODI. Nevertheless, there are still discrepancies between China's official statistics and other data sets, for instance when compared to statistics from UNCTAD World Investment Reports. Moreover, when statistics from the Chinese Ministry of Commerce have been compared with statistics put out by the Hong Kong government concerning China's outbound FDI, the Hong Kong statistics have presented a higher rate of ODI to Hong Kong alone than China's official statistics give for its total ODI to the entire world. Trade mis-invoicing, capital flight and smuggling may account for some of the discrepancies and are reasons why such statistics cannot be fully relied upon. Indeed, the ability to move revenues, sometimes including state assets, abroad has been an additional 'push factor' for Chinese overseas investment, allowing some officials and managers to enrich themselves and their families and to emigrate overseas[20]. Fear of capital flight is one reason why China introduced restrictions on some forms of "irrational" investment, despite its overall desire to expand overseas investment, in 2016.

Despite the limits of the statistics, they can nevertheless be useful for giving us indications of some general trends. Most significantly, China's overseas investment has grown incredibly since it first implemented its 'going global' strategy from the early 2000s. Whereas in 2002, Chinese investors only spent US$2.7 billion on overseas acquisitions and greenfield projects, by 2013 this amount had increased to US$108 billion[21]. Having taken off further from the mid-2000s, and then following the announcement of plans for the BRI in 2013, China's Outbound FDI continued to grow substantially prior to 2017. According to official statistics in 2015, China became a net exporter of capital for the first time, when its ODI flow increased to US$145.7 billion overtaking inbound FDI to the country of US$135.6[22].

In 2017, ODI began to decline. This can be attributed to the introduction of restrictions on "irrational" investments by the Chinese government, some overseas countries beginning to adopt a more cautious attitude towards Chinese ODI and tensions arising over the US-China trade war. Having risen to become widely reported as the world's second largest source of FDI in 2016, for the first half of 2019 China was only the fifth largest source according to OECD data[23]. Notably it has been ODI into developed markets in Europe and North America that has seen the sharpest decline (by 73% in 2018), while ODI to BRI countries actually saw an increase of 8.9% that year[24]. For now, however, China's overall ODI remains very significant even if it has fallen from its peak, although the impact of the Covid-19 pandemic makes for a very uncertain future.

Globally, developed economies along with Hong Kong and tax havens such as the Cayman Islands and the Virgin Islands, have been among the top major recipient countries of Chinese ODI, although developing countries and regions have increasingly been receiving a greater percentage. This is something which might perhaps be expected to continue if further infrastructure development and related investments are pursued in line with the BRI. Meanwhile Hong Kong has for a longtime retained its position as by far the largest recipient of mainland outbound FDI, although its share of Chinese total ODI stock fell 6% between 2015 when the BRI was implemented and the end of 2017.

Interestingly, it is Latin America, a region not initially included as a part of the BRI initiative, that had seen the greatest recent growth by the end of 2017 as a percentage of China's total stock ODI. This growth in the total share of ODI stock in Latin America, mostly appears to be at the expense of the share of ODI in Asia. Although Hong Kong as by far the largest recipient, is the location where this is most notable, the share of Asia excluding Hong Kong also fell from 10% at the end of 2015 to 9.5% at the end of 2016 and to 8.7% at the end of 2017. Nevertheless, the monetary value of ODI to each world region, including Asia, has continued to rise in this period. While the statistics presented above would seemingly illustrate that Latin America has become more important from a global perspective for Chinese overseas investment, this does not necessarily mean that Asia has become less so. The launching and continued promotion of the BRI initiative would suggest the otherwise. Moreover, on looking more closely at Chinese ODI in Latin America, it is noticeable that the majority of Chinese ODI to the region in fact goes to just two locations: the Cayman Islands and the Virgin Islands. Both are considered tax havens. These two locations accounted for 65.5% and 31.5% respectively of Chinese stock ODI in Latin America at the end of 2017.

Initially, the majority of China's overseas investment involved SOEs, however private capital has also been encouraged to invest overseas since 1998. In 2006, 81% of Chinese outward stock FDI belonged to SOEs while private enterprises only accounted for 1%[25]. The private sector has increasingly been more active in investment overseas. In 2018, head of the All-China Federation of Industry and Commerce, Gao Yunlong, reported that more than 60% of China's fixed-asset investment and outbound investment had been made by private investors[26].

Nevertheless, it is China's major SOEs that have been key players in building and implementing infrastructure projects overseas, and China's state-owned financial institutions that have provided significant financing to support such overseas development projects that fulfil the aims of the BRI. By 2018, more than 80 of 96 enterprises owned by the Chinese central government had taken part in 3,100 BRI investment projects over the preceding five years[27]. Indeed, there has also been significant expansion in overseas lending as well as the number of projects contracted to Chinese companies overseas.

ODI is not the only form of investment related economic activity that has expanded along with the BRI. Infrastructure projects frequently take a form where the receiving country obtains Chinese financing for the project, and then construction or other forms of implementation are contracted out to a Chinese company (sometimes as terms of the financing agreement). Indeed, 89% of Chinese funded BRI projects have Chinese contractors[28] and the value of Chinese overseas contracts has been something which has risen rapidly since the early twenty-first century. Moreover, overseas contracts are also worth commenting on as they sometimes total more than the value of China's non-financial direct investment. In the first four months of 2018, for instance, China's non-financial investment to BRI countries was $4.67 billion (a 17.3% increase compared to the same period the previous year), while the volume of overseas contracted projects was US$24.2 billion, an increase of 27.7%[29]. According to official statistics, Asia awards the greatest proportion of the total value of projects contracted to Chinese companies overseas, accounting for 48% of the total in 2016.

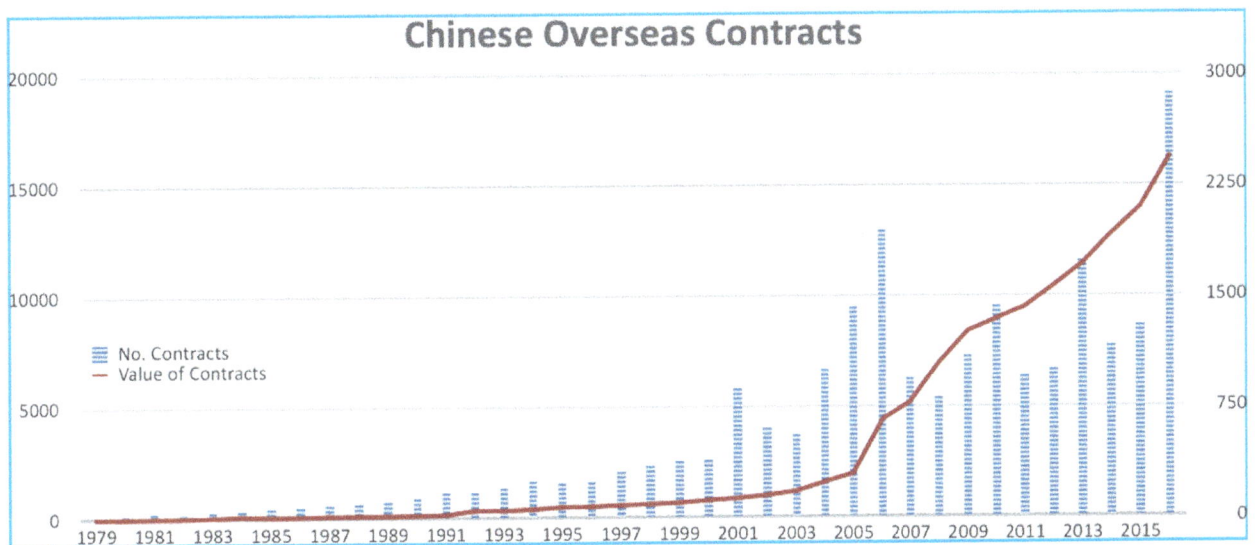

Based on data from the China Statistical Yearbook 2017

While Chinese companies have long been contractors for construction projects (often financed by Chinese banks such as the China Development Bank and Export-Import Bank of China), more recently an increasing number of Chinese SOEs are also operating and investing in these projects, for instance through a Build-Operate-Transfer (BOT) model[30], by taking an equity share in the project that it constructs, or even through a model where it owns and operates the project that it constructs indefinitely[31].

Having previously been a major recipient of ADB financing, China's cross-border lending is something which has grown in significance with the launch of BRI, since many Chinese banks are responsible for providing loans to finance associated infrastructure investments in BRI countries and are therefore important for ensuring its viability. The loans provided vary in nature, from those that are interest free to loans repayable at fully commercial rates, however exact information on the details and scale are often difficult to obtain as the Chinese banks, as well as debtor countries, often do not report them in a systematic manner or disclose full details of agreements.

It should be noted that Chinese lending sometimes mistakenly gets classified as aid or development assistance. While China does provide some grants and soft loans that might be classified as aid, it generally does not distinguish between the different type of financial flows; what is often described as aid does not always meet OECD criteria for aid (also defined as Official Development Assistance or ODA)[32]. This lack of distinction means that China is sometimes presented as one of the world's largest donors, whereas in reality this might be a dubious claim. According to a 2017 study by AidData, between 2000 and 2014, China gave or lent $350 billion; $75 billion was grants or concessional lending but the remainder consisted of non-concessional loans (US aid was $424bn almost all concessional and/or in the form of grants). The same study found that China's non-concessional lending has not impacted on recipient countries' GDP and instead appears to act as subsidies for Chinese companies, as well as to benefit local elites[33].

How is Overseas Investment is shaped by the Chinese government?

The policies of the Chinese government have played a significant role in shaping and guiding the expansion of Chinese investment overseas since it began encouraging Chinese companies to invest overseas. This means that activities have not only been directed towards the economic interests of the Chinese party-state, but also towards fulfilling its political interests.

Outbound investment (state and private) is regulated by various governmental bodies and subject to relevant government guidelines and regulations. Prior to 2014, all outbound investment required approval by the National Development and Reform Commission (NDRC) or the Ministry of Commerce (MOFCOM). In early 2014, coinciding with the beginning of the BRI era, the Chinese government liberalised regulation on outbound direct investments, such that most investment was only required to be registered. Approval was still required for investments to "sensitive" countries or in "sensitive" sectors, which included large-scale land and resource development, telecommunications, and media[34].

Since November 2016, however, the Chinese government began to tighten controls once more. This has included stricter control over offshore remittances of funds and restricting transactions financed by foreign currency loans from outside of China and secured by onshore assets and Renminbi funds. Following these controls, a 46% decline in outbound direct investment was recorded by MOFCOM in the first half of 2017[35]. Then, in August 2017, the Opinions on Further Guiding and Regulating Outbound Investment (the Guidelines) were jointly issued by the National Development and Reform Commission, the Ministry of Commerce, the People's Bank of China and the Ministry of Foreign Affairs. The Guidelines classify overseas investments into three categories; encouraged, restricted and prohibited investments. Belt and Road investments are amongst those which companies were encouraged to invest in, along with investments that support production capacity, strengthen high-tech cooperation and cooperation in agriculture. Meanwhile investments in real estate, hotels, entertainment and sports clubs were restricted, and investments involving export of military industrial technology, gambling or investments that may harm China's national interests were prohibited.

These new restrictions and scrutiny of overseas investments by the Chinese government further curbed some overseas investment activities and led some divestment. The Dalian Wanda Group and its investments in the entertainment industry in the US and Europe is one of the more high profile examples of a company to come under increased scrutiny by the Chinese government and to be hit by new restrictions, which it was found to have breached, prompting it to sell off over US$9 billion of its assets. Other companies placed on China's watch list have included the Anbang Group, HNA Group, Fosun Group and CEFC China[36].

This issue of capital flight has become a growing concern for the Chinese government, prompting some of the increased restrictions and stronger capital controls that have led to a decline in and cancellation of some overseas investment deals, especially non-BRI investments. Nevertheless, as the Panama papers revealed, current and former top leaders in China are amongst those who have moved their wealth abroad through the ownership of offshore companies. At the same time that capital flight may be a primary concern, the poor reputation and growing backlash against some of China's overseas investments might provide an additional reason for the introduction of tighter restrictions at a time that China has upgraded the political importance of its investments overseas.

Risky business

The behaviour of Chinese companies operating overseas has been widely criticized for either having little awareness of or acting in disregard of local laws and regulations, thereby sometimes resulting or contributing to labour rights violations and environmental destruction. Over the years, the Chinese government, increasingly aware of the bad reputation surrounding Chinese investors, has issued a number of (often non-binding) guidelines and, to an increasing extent, regulations that partially cover these issues to promote better practice by Chinese companies operating overseas.

One example is the issuing of the "Nine Principles" to "Encourage and Standardise Enterprises Overseas Investment" by the Chinese State Council in 2005. The principles say that Chinese companies operating overseas should abide by local laws, bid for contracts on the basis of transparency and equality, protect the labour rights of local employees, protect the environment and implement Corporate Social Responsibility[37]. More recently in late 2017, in line with the increasing attempts to regulate Chinese investment activities overseas, the government issued a Code of Conduct for Overseas Investment by Private Enterprises, while in March 2018 the new Administrative Measures for Overseas Investments by Enterprises came into effect, notably expanding, amongst other aspects, the scope of earlier measures such that they also applied to Hong Kong, Macau and Taiwan enterprises controlled by domestic enterprises or persons. Although sometimes lacking in explicit mention of labour rights, such regulations and guidelines do consistently require that legal requirements be met, social responsibilities fulfilled, and the environment protected.

In addition to infringements of local laws and standards, in some instances risky or ill planned investments have also led to a failure to deliver, and some Chinese companies and projects have fallen through. This not only has the potential to contribute to a poor reputation in the country concerned, risky investments are also potentially economically detrimental from a Chinese perspective. In 2015 even official Chinese media reported that, "a large portion of China's current investment abroad have failed to meet expectations, as they are either stalled, over schedule or suffering financial losses"[38] and that since 2005 more than US$250 billion in overseas investment had failed. Indeed, according to Chu Yu, a professor at the University of International Relations, Chinese banks have, "limited experience in assessing the risks in foreign-related projects", compared to US, European and Japanese banks and this is one reason why they may charge higher interest rates[39]. Potentially higher interest rates of course heighten risks that some countries may suffer from debt distress.

This report

In view of the potential limitations and risks from China's overseas investment strategy, this report aims to look at some of the key issues that have emerged following the upgrading of the political significance of Chinese overseas investment to the Chinese party-state that was signaled with the launch of the BRI. After first providing a brief overview of the routes of the Belt and Road themselves, the rest of this report considers two important mechanisms which have aided China's investment overseas and its international expansion – its financial institutions and the Hong Kong Special Administrative Region. It also examines three examples of strategic Chinese companies that have significant overseas investment and then focuses on China's investments in the Belt and Road regions of Asia, Africa and an example from Europe (Germany). In providing an overview of some of the issues involved related to these aspects of Chinese overseas investment and the consequences for recipient countries and the people and environment, it is hoped that awareness can be raised with a view to coordinating further discussion amongst civil society and developing tools to assist environmental protection, the defense of the rights of those negatively impacted, and the search for viable alternatives.

Part 2: Spotlight on Belt and Road Routes

The BRI is comprised of six land based economic corridors as well as the 21st Century Maritime Silk Road. The 6 Economic Corridors include:

1. The New Eurasian Land Bridge
2. The China - Mongolia - Russia Corridor
3. The China - Central Asia - West Asia Corridor
4. The China - Indochina Peninsula Corridor
5. The China – Pakistan Economic Corridor
6. The Bangladesh - China - India - Myanmar Corridor

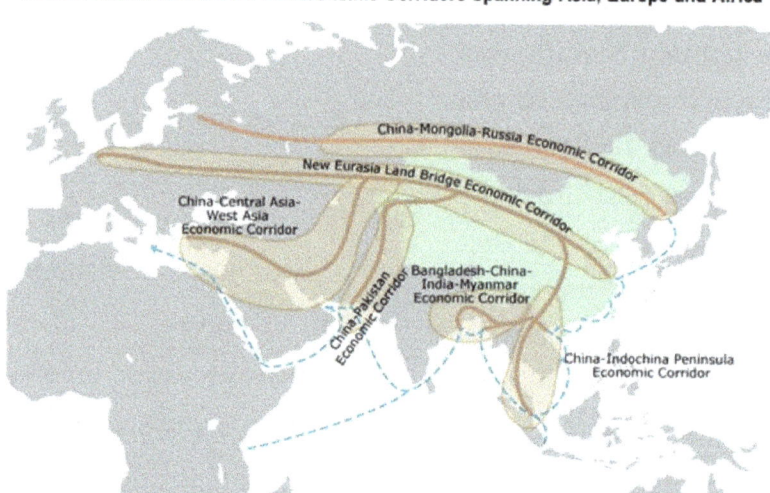

The Belt and Road Initiative: Six Economic Corridors Spanning Asia, Europe and Africa

1. The New Eurasian Land Bridge

The New Eurasian Land Bridge refers to a series of railway lines running for approximately 7,500 miles (12,000 kilometres), or further (for instance on the route to Madrid), connecting China and Europe. There is some degree of variation to the exact routes that supposedly form a part of this connection, which comprises existing (prior to the BRI) as well as newly constructed railroads. However, the connection is generally said to involve the rail link between Yiwu in Zhejiang province, Eastern China, and Duisburg in Germany; Yiwu and Madrid in Spain or Yiwu and London in the UK (since January 2017), although Chinese official media has sometimes described the route as running from Lianyuangang in Jiangsu (also Eastern China) to Rotterdam in the Netherlands. The journey from China to Europe takes about two weeks, passing through Kazakhstan and Russia, and is used for the transportation of freight.

There has been a remarkable rise in intermodal rail freight traffic between China and Europe since the launch of the BRI. In November 2018, China Railway Corporation (CRC) reported that more than 3000 container trains had travelled between China and Europe since 2017, exceeding the total number that had run between these destinations in the previous six years combined[40]. Nevertheless, the corridor has been criticized for lacking economic sense. It is more expensive than sea transportation, lacks climate control and more than half of the containers return to China empty as there is a big disparity between eastbound and westbound freight[41]. The route also suffers from a break of gauge along the route between the standard gauge used in China and Europe and the Russian gauge used in CIS states, which means that containers have to be physically transferred using truck mounted cranes between railway cars at the China-Kazakh border and again at the Belarus-Poland border[42].

Duisburg Intermodal Terminal (DIT) container terminal at the end of the Chongqing-Duisburg route. Photo: Globalization Monitor.

2. The China - Mongolia – Russia Economic Corridor

The aim of this corridor is to strengthen trade between China, Russia and Mongolia by modernising infrastructure connections and developing Mongolia as a hub linking China and Russia. Adopted in 2016, the three countries agreed to implement 32 projects under its framework. Amongst major planned projects is the China-Mongolia Cross-border Economic Cooperation Zone, a zone which covers from Erenhot in Inner Mongolia, China, to Zamiin Uud in southeastern Mongolia (9 square kilometres on each side of the border). In September 2017, China 22MCC Group, an SOE that is a wholly-owned subsidiary of super conglomerate China Metallurgical Group Corporation (MCC), signed an agreement to construct infrastructure on the Chinese side consisting of underground pipelines, office buildings, roads and plants, and to operate the facilities for 13 years after the completion of construction. Total investment in the project was US$125 million dollars. It was expected to take two years to complete[43]. However, in July 2019, a China Daily report quotes the deputy director of Erenhot's bureau of commerce as saying that, "We plan to complete the construction of the 3-square km core area by 2020"[44]. Another major project for the corridor is the Northern Railway Corridor which aims to extend the rail network connecting Mongolia with Russia and China. A long-discussed initiative, the railway will also facilitate the sending of mining products from Russia to China and finished goods from China to Russia.

Source: Global Infrastructure Connectivity Alliance

Many of the plans for the corridor are yet to be completed and some delays have been reported in its progress, for instance concerning some of the proposed rail routes. Meanwhile old plans that had yet to be implemented have been renewed. One example concerns the construction of a highway bridge across the River Amur connecting Hebei in northeastern China to Blagoveshchensk in Russia's Far East (previously the crossing could only be made by ferry). The agreement to construct the bridge had originally been signed in 1995 but little progress was made, and it subsequently became incorporated into the BRI as a flagship project. Construction officially began in 2016 and was scheduled for completion by October 2019, however a report from The Diplomat from late 2018 found that most locals were unaware of the bridge and that progress was seemingly slow, especially on the Russian side[45]. Nevertheless, one year later, Russian officials reported that the bridge had been completed and would open in 2020. The bridge is intended to increase freight traffic and agricultural products transported between the two countries[46].

For Mongolia, despite slow progress in some areas along this corridor, in 2019, when Chinese Premier Li Keqiang met with President Khaaltma Battugla of Mongolia, commitments to advance the construction of the Mongolia-China-Russia Economic Corridor were again emphasized[47]. As a landlocked country, investment in road and rail infrastructure is potential very advantageous to Mongolia. Nevertheless, a potential danger for overreliance on China has been identified, with around 80% of Mongolia's export volumes (mostly copper, coal and gold) already going to China[48].

3. The China-Central Asia-West Asia Economic Corridor (CCWAEC)

The CCWAEC: source OBOReurope

The CCWAEC is central to the new Silk Road and is significant for largely following the path of the ancient Silk Road, linking China and the Arabian Peninsula. It starts from Xinjiang in China and crosses five Central Asian countries (Kazakhstan, Kyrgyzstan, Tajikistan, Uzbekistan and Turkmenistan) and 17 countries and regions in West Asia (including Iran, Saudi Arab and Turkey)[49]. The significance of Central Asia for the BRI was evident when Kazakhstan was chosen as the location for Xi Jinping to first announce plans for the initiative in 2013.

The route is significant as it crosses the natural resource rich Central and West Asia region. Developing infrastructure therefore helps to facilitate transportation of these resources. Indeed, a major aspect of plans for the corridor include road and railway construction. There are also geopolitical implications however; not only has Russia historically been a prominent player in Central Asia but, especially considering the resource richness of the region, the United States is also another competitor with an interest. Exerting greater influence in a region at its border in view of these two significant competitors may be advantageous to China.

Some projects such as the Wahdat-Yovon railroad in Tajikistan and the Angren-

Pap Tunnel in Uzbekistan, both of which were built by Chinese railway construction companies have already been completed and opened to traffic[50]. Nevertheless, despite the importance of this corridor to the new Silk Road, a 2018 research paper published by the Development Research Centre for China's State Council found that construction of the corridor was difficult to push forward rapidly due to national and objective conditions of Central Asian and West Asian countries[51].

4. The China-Indochina Peninsula Economic Corridor (CICPEC).

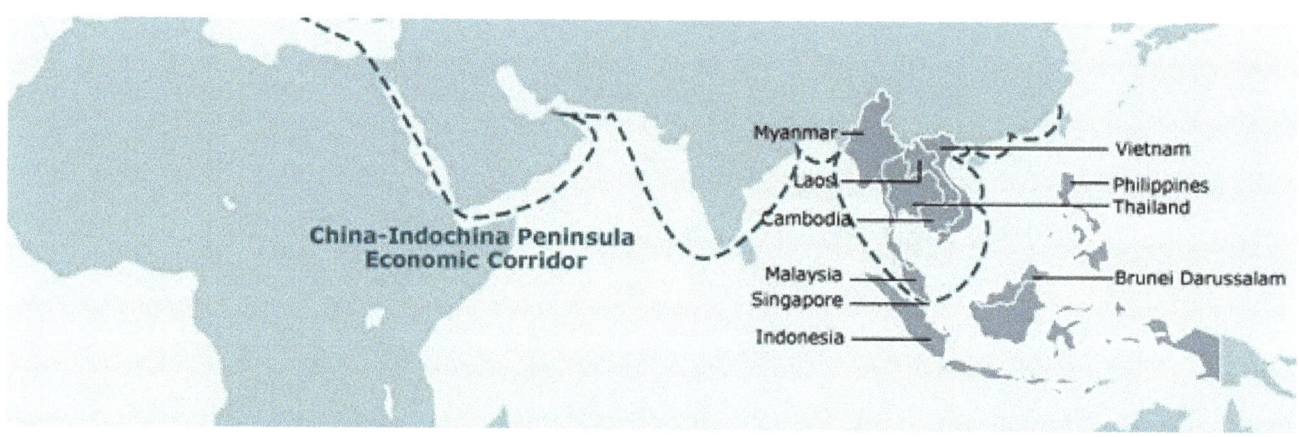

The China-Indochina Peninsula Economic Corridor. Source: HKTDC

The Indochina economic corridor connects ASEAN countries, thereby acting to further regional integration in Southeast Asia. In this respect, it represents a continuation of China's push towards greater trade with ASEAN countries. Already in 2010, the China-ASEAN Free Trade Area (CAFTA) was launched and bilateral trade has been growing significantly since then. Between 2009 and 2014 it increased at an average annual rate of 18%[52]. A deal to upgrade the CAFTA, covering areas including goods, services, investment, and economic and technological cooperation with the aim of increasing bilateral trade to 1 trillion US dollars by 2020 was then signed by China and ASEAN in November 2015.

As in the case of the other economic corridors, many existing projects in the countries concerned have been reclassified under the umbrella of this project. One example is the Preah Vihear-Kaoh Kong Railyway in Cambodia. Plans for this 405 kilometre railway line date back to at least 2010 when the China Railway Group and Cambodia Iron and Steel Mining Industry Group (CISMIG) announced a joint venture to build a line connecting a planned steel factory in Preah Vihear with a new port in the Gulf of Thailand[53]. In 2013, the project, which was described as the, "biggest infrastructure project in Cambodia's history", received criticism from locals and civil society due to lack of publicly available information and dialogue as well as concerns about the potential negative impacts on locals of mining activities carried out by CISMIG connected to the project[54]. Although the plan then subsequently stalled due to funding problems, it was picked up again with the BRI and classified as part of the CICPEC.

Within China, Yunnan and Guangxi, both provinces that border Southeast Asian countries, play a significant role for the CICPEC. The planned Nanning-Pingxiang high-speed railway line in Guangxi province is seen as a step to facilitate this corridor, as the route will go on to connect with railway lines in Vietnam and eventually to a network that will extend to Singapore. The Nanning to Chongzuo section of the line is expected to open in 2021[55].

5. The China-Pakistan Economic Corridor (CPEC)

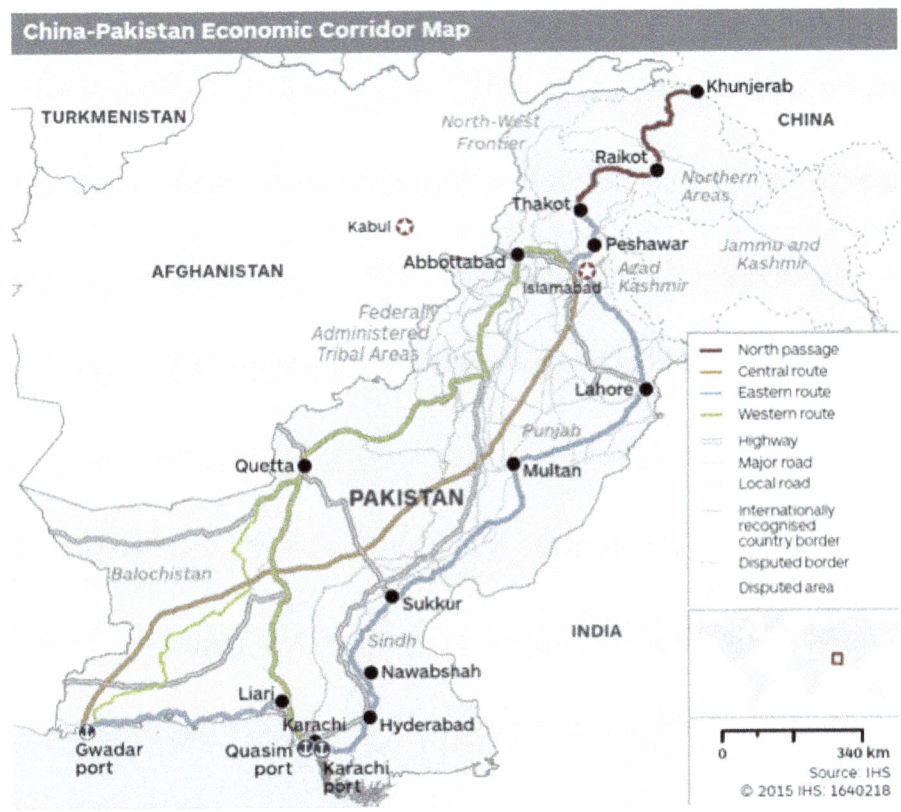

Source: Journal of Commerce

Initial plans for the China-Pakistan Economic Corridor (CPEC) predate those of the BRI, however they have been revitalized and given renewed impetus under it. The corridor, which involves a series of infrastructure projects linking the two countries, runs for 3,000 kilometres from Kashgar in western China to the port of Gwadar in Pakistan. Along the corridor huge infrastructure projects, including roads, railways and power plants and an optical cable fibre network are either being planned or built and largely funded by Chinese capital and loans. The further development of Gwadar Port, a deep water sea-port, which lies at the end of the corridor is one important component (see Part 7 for further details). In addition to infrastructure and transportation networks, the plan for CPEC also involves agriculture projects.

The total value of the CPEC projects was estimated to be US$62 billion in 2017. While the corridor provides many potential opportunities for Chinese enterprises and facilitates China's access to resources and transportation networks, and Pakistan's government has also promoted it as beneficial to Pakistan, CPEC has been widely criticized for the risks that it potentially poses to Pakistan, especially concerning the debt burdens it may pose and the risk of leaving it trapped in a state of dependency on China. Concerns for people and the environment have also been raised including those related to displacement, negative impacts on livelihoods, destruction of farmland and expansion of coal power[56]. At the same time, the security risks involved with the corridor also pose threats to some of its projects and those working on them (both local and Chinese workers).

6. The Bangladesh - China - India - Myanmar Corridor (BCIM)

This 2,800km corridor aims to connect Kunming in the East of China with Kolkata via Dhaka in Bangladesh and Mandalay in Myanmar. It aims to strengthen transportation and infrastructure networks and to increases interregional trade.

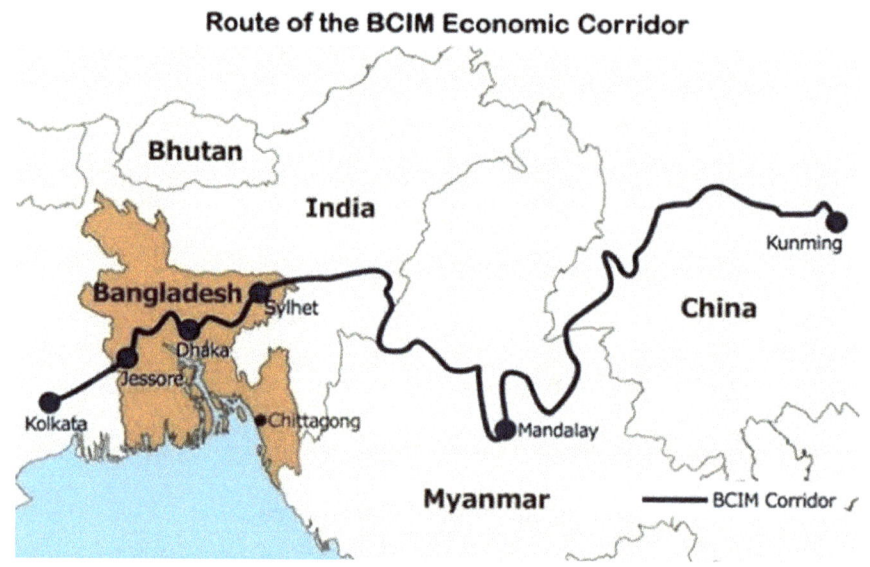

Source: Belt and Road News

The corridor faces significant barriers to its progress due to tensions between China and India, however. Despite this corridor involving India, it is important to note that India has never firmly committed to the BRI. Indeed, with the CPEC passing through disputed Kashmir, the BRI has been a source of tension between China and India on top of existing territorial and economic rivalries.

In 2019, following China's second Belt and Road summit (which India did not attend), it was reported that this corridor might have been dropped from the list of projects under the BRI, as it was not included in the list of projects in the annex of the summit's Joint Communique of the Leaders' Roundtable[57]. Despite this, plans for a BCIM itself have not been entirely dropped and India did attend the 13th BCIM forum in Kunming later in the year. Indeed, it would seem that India sees some degree of economic importance to the corridor and may simply not want it to be a China dominated project. India has also reportedly taken the view that as the BCIM predates the BRI it cannot be a part of it[58].

The New Maritime Silk Road (MSR)

The MSR aims to transform deep-sea trade from southern China to Southeast Asia through to Africa and Europe. Like the Silk Road Economic Belt, the MSR involves infrastructure development, only this time it is sea based and it involves ports and shipyards. The original plan aims for the MSR to consist of three "blue economic passages": the China-Indian Ocean-Africa-Mediterranean Sea Blue Economic Passage, the China-Oceania-South Pacific Blue Economic Passage, and a passage to Europe via the Arctic Ocean. In addition to the development of trade, an additional advantage of the MSR is to protect China's control over key sea trade routes and to guarantee uninterrupted import of raw materials.

One difference that has been highlighted between the MSR and the Silk Road Economic Belt is that MSR routes have largely been operating for a long time (although construction and expansion of more ports along these routes is planned), whereas the land-based roads and railways required for the SREB corridors are less developed[59].

The New Maritime Silk Road was first announced by Xi Jinping in Indonesia in 2013, and for China, Southeast Asia is an especially important region for the MSR in furthering regional connectivity as well as its geopolitical influence. The establishment of a Maritime Silk Road Investment Fund and a Maritime Silk Road Bank to help fund Maritime Silk Road projects have also been mentioned in literature discussing the Maritime Silk Road.

The Silk Road Extended

While the six economic corridors and maritime silk road were all parts of the BRI when it was first launched, China has since extended the application of the term Silk Road to broader ambitions. In 2018, for instance, the Chinese government presented the idea of a Polar Silk Road in its White Paper on Arctic Policy[60]. The paper states that China hopes to work with other BRI parties to develop Arctic shipping routes and that it encourages its companies to participate in infrastructure construction for these routes. While the paper also presents the intention of working with Arctic states to explore clean energy in the region, it nevertheless encourages Chinese companies to participate in the exploration of oil, gas and mineral resources, ("on the condition of properly protecting the eco-environment of the Arctic") thereby continuing to expand polluting forms of energy.

The application of the Silk Road even extends beyond the land and sea. It has also launched a Space Silk Road with the aim of BRI states subscribing to use of China's Beidou satellites for precision navigation and timing. Meanwhile the Digital Silk Road aims to expand China's role as a global provider of digital infrastructure.

Part 3: Financing China's Investments Overseas

Having previously itself been a major recipient of ADB financing, China's own cross-border lending has continued to grow in significance with the launch of the BRI. Indeed, many Chinese banks and financial institutions are responsible for providing loans to finance infrastructure investments in BRI, as well as other, countries and are therefore important for ensuring the initiative's viability. The loans provided vary in nature, from those that are interest free to loans repayable at fully commercial rates. However exact information on the details and scale of lending are often difficult to obtain as the Chinese banks, as well as debtor countries, often do not report them in a systematic manner or disclose full details of agreements.

It should be noted that Chinese lending sometimes mistakenly gets classified as aid or development assistance[61]. While China does provide grants and soft loans that might be classified as aid, it generally does not distinguish between different types of financial flows. This means that what is often described as aid does not always meet OECD criteria for aid (also defined as Official Development Assistance or ODA)[62]. This lack of distinction means that China is sometimes presented as one of the world's largest donors, whereas in reality this might be a dubious claim. According to a 2017 study by AidData, between 2000 and 2014, China gave or lent US$350 billion. While US$75 billion was in the form of grants or concessional lending, the remainder consisted of non-concessional loans[63]. Many of these non-concessional loans may have higher interest rates and shorter maturities and have commodity revenues as collateral[64]. The AidData study also found that China's non-concessional lending has not impacted on recipient countries' GDP and instead appeared to have acted as subsidies for Chinese companies, as well as to benefit local elites[65]. In other words, these loans are not necessarily benefiting the countries concerned beyond the local elites, although many loans are beneficial to the interests of Chinese companies operating overseas. According to another report, outstanding loans to China by overseas countries amount to more than US$700 billion today. Moreover, half of loans to developing countries are "hidden", meaning that the World Bank and IMF do not have data on them[66].

Financial institutions

Various Chinese or Chinese initiated financial institutions have been utilised by the Chinese government and Chinese companies for projects associated with overseas investment and economic activities, including those related to the Belt and Road initiative. These include new multilateral institutions initiated by China, Chinese policy banks, Chinese state-owned commercial banks, state backed investment funds and other investment companies. The following section provides short profiles of some of these institutions and their significance for Chinese overseas investment activities.

Policy banks

The policy banks, especially the China Development Bank (CDB) and the Export-Import Bank of China (Exim) have been the leading institutions operating overseas in support of the 'going out strategy' and have been China's main source of overseas lending. Under the direct jurisdiction of the State Council, China's policy banks were established in 1994 with the aim of advancing China's economic policies.

Since the announcement of the BRI, the Chinese government has injected significant amounts of additional capital into both CDB and Exim. Already, by the end of 2016, these two banks had together provided $200 billion in loans to the BRI[67].

China Development Bank (CDB)

The CDB is China's largest overseas lender. By the end of 2018, the bank had a total foreign-currency denominated loan balance equivalent to US$250 billion and cross-border RMB loan balance of 95.7 billion[68].

Founded as a policy bank to support China's economic goals, CDB was incorporated as China Development Bank Corporation in 2008. It is a Global Fortune 500 company. As of 2018, its main shareholders were the Chinese Ministry of Finance (36.54%), Central Huijin Investment Ltd (an SOE) (34.68%), Buttonwood Investment Holding Company Ltd (a company solely funded by the state administration of foreign exchange) (27.19%), and the National Council for Social Security Fund (1.59%). The bank raises capital by issuing bonds to institutional investors and foreign markets[69] and has been a major lender supporting development and infrastructure projects domestically and internationally.

It now describes itself as the world's largest development finance institution[70], and has stated that it has the leading position among Chinese banks in terms of overseas financing. Besides 41 branches in the Chinese mainland, CDB has considerable international presence with branches or representative offices in HK, Cairo, Moscow, Rio de Janeiro, Caracas, London, Vientiane, Astana, Minsk, Jakarta and Sydney. One of its subsidiaries, the China-Africa Development Fund (CAD Fund), was established in 2007 and was the first Chinese equity fund dedicated to investments in Africa. Another international initiative by CDB in Africa is the Investing in Africa Think Tank Alliance (IATTA), which it initiated in 2015 with the endorsement of the World Bank and several countries in Africa to support investment and development in Africa.

In line with advancing China's policies towards expanding investments overseas, following the announcement of the BRI in 2013, CDB planned to reserve more than US$890 billion for the development of more than 900 BRI projects. In 2016 it provided loans totalling US$12.6 billion to support the BRI, especially targeting infrastructure connectivity, production capacity, equipment manufacturing and overseas industrial parks. Nevertheless, the bank's lending so far to support the BRI, while significant, has still been substantially less than initially pledged. By the end of 2017, it had so far lent a total of US$110 billion to BRI countries, and by the end of 2018 it claimed to have made an equivalent of RMB466.5 billion loan commitments[71].

In considering the banks international lending overall, it should also be noted that despite its significant overseas lending, in 2018 locations "outside the Chinese Mainland" accounted for only 2.25% of CDB's outstanding net loan balance[72]. In other words, this amounted to only a tiny fraction in comparison to domestic loans. Amongst recent notable projects, in 2018, CDB provided loans to support the Zhuhai link road of the Hong Kong-Zhuhai-Macau Bridge, the Shymkent Oil Refineries Upgrading Project in Kazakhstan, the Hengyi Pulau Muara Besar Petrochemical Project in Brunei and the Jakarta-Bundang High-speed Rail in Indonesia. It is also notable that Venezuela, has been loaned a significant proportion of CDB overseas loans (US$40 billion between 2008 and 2013), with much of the lending based on oil for loans agreements[73].

As an institution designed to advance Chinese state policy, representatives from the bank have sometimes by quoted as saying that it is not seeking to maximise profits[74]. However, in discussing lending to BRI projects, then CDB Chairman, Hu Huaibang, was reported to have stated that profitability was the first criterion when assessing which projects to fund[75].

CDB has also been linked to a major corruption case. In July 2019, then CDB Chairman, Hu Huaibing, was place under investigation for serious violations of Communist Party discipline in what has become one of China's most high profile recent anti-corruption cases in the financial sector. Ha had only recently stepped down as Chairman in September of the previous year. In January 2020 he was expelled from the Chinese Communist Party and in February he was arrested. According to Chinese media reports, Hu had helped fuel the rise of two Chinese conglomerates, CEFC China Energy Co. Ltd. and HNA Group Co. Ltd, by helping obtain billions of dollars in dubious credit. CEFC's credit driven expansion saw the energy company amass a wide range of assets around the world, including in Europe, Asia, Africa and the Middle East[76]. CEFC's Chairman Ye Jianming was placed under investigation for economic crimes in 2018 and the company was declared bankrupt in April 2020.

The Export-Import Bank of China (Exim)

Like CDB, Exim bank of China is under the jurisdiction of the State Council and designed to further the Chinese government's economic goals. Unlike CDB, which supports China's economic and social development strategies more generally, Exim's focus is more specifically to support China's foreign trade, investment and international economic cooperation.

In addition to 32 branches in mainland China, it has a representative office in Hong Kong, a branch in Paris, and representative offices for Southern and Eastern Africa, St. Petersburg and Northern and Western Africa. Its main shareholders are the Ministry of Finance (10.74%) and Buttonwood Investment Company Ltd. (89.26%).

In 2018, the bank had an outstanding balance of foreign trade loans of RMB10765.28 hundred million, an outstanding balance of cross-border investment loans of RMB2725.65 hundred million, an outstanding balance of international cooperation loans of RMB8861.78 hundred million, and an outstanding balance of loans for supporting greater openness of RMB11398.99 hundred million[77].

In 2016, the bank described its aim as giving priority to the BRI and supporting China's efforts to, "build a community of shared destiny with its neighbours", continuing to provide loans to African countries, boosting cooperation with Europe (especially Central and Eastern Europe), and continuing to explore US and Latin American markets. Among major projects that the bank has recently helped to finance include the Abuja Light Rail in Nigeria (West Africa's first light rail), the Kampala-Entebbe Airport Expressway in Uganda, the Hanoi Urban Railway, the Jujuy Photovoltaic Power Plant Project in Argentina, the China-Railway Express (helping to transport freight from Central Asia and Europe) and the Hong Kong-Zhuhai-Macao Bridge.

The bank is also the, "designated institution to implement the Chinese Government Concessional Loan and Preferential Export Buyer's Credit". According to the bank's annual report, by the end of 2018 the bank's concessional business covered 90 countries in the ASEAN, South Asia, Central Asia, West Asia, Africa, Latin America and the South Pacific, helping to improve infrastructure, the investment environment and living standards[78].

In view of the potentially heavy debt burden resulting from substantial banks loans, Exim has reportedly imposed a debt ceiling for each BRI country. Indeed Sun Ping, Vice Governor of Exim, is reported as having said, "For some countries, if we give them too many loans, too much debt, then the sustainability of its debt is questionable"[79]. Nevertheless, the bank has lent money to projects in countries experiencing significant debt issues, for instance to Zambia.

State –owned commercial banks

China's state-owned commercial banks (especially the "big four": the Bank of China, Industrial and Commercial Bank of China (ICBC), Agricultural Bank of China, China Construction Bank) are also financing and have agreements related to BRI projects. Many of the commercial banks have expanded the number of overseas branches and offices in recent years coinciding with the BRI. Already, by the end of 2016, China's three largest state-owned commercial banks were reported to have lent US$225.4 billion to BRI projects[80]. Nevertheless, these banks differ to the policy banks in that funding is entirely commercial. According to ICBC president, Gu Shu, "If we do not do these projects on commercial terms, it will be unsustainable and we cannot be a part of it." By September

2017, this bank was taking part in 212 BRI projects with credit facilities exceeding US$67 billion[81]. Some of these banks have been more cautious about their overseas investments and hesitant to take on overseas projects alone[82].

State-backed Investment Funds and Companies

In addition to loans from the policy banks and commercial banks, the Chinese Government has also set up or backed several funds to support overseas investment and the BRI. The Silk Road Fund is amongst the most high-profile funds set up specifically to support the BRI. It was established in December 2014 with investment from the State Administration of Foreign Exchange (65%), the Export-Import Bank of China (15%), the China Investment Corporation (15%) and the China Development Bank (5%). The fund, which started with a total capacity of US$40 billion[83], supports, "infrastructure, resources and energy development, industrial capacity cooperation and financial cooperation in countries and regions involved in the Belt and Road Initiative"[84]. The fund's first overseas investment was agreed in 2015 and concerned investment in the Karot Hydropower Project and other projects as part of CPEC in Pakistan.

The China-ASEAN Investment Cooperation Fund (CAF) is another fund that is expected to provide increasing support to the BRI. Established in 2010, the fund targets investment in infrastructure, energy and natural resources, and China aims for it to help deepen cooperation between itself and ASEAN countries. China's Exim bank was the main sponsor contributing the most starting capital to the fund, but other investors, including the World' Bank's IFC, have also contributed to and hold equity in the fund.

Other funds include the China Insurance Investment Fund, the Silk Road Gold Fund, the China-Central and Eastern Europe Investment Cooperation Fund, the China-Africa Fund for Industrial Cooperation, and the Green Ecological Silk Road Fund to name just a few.

In addition to the funds mentioned above, support for China's overseas investment strategies including the BRI have also come from investment companies such as the CITIC Group. The CITIC group was founded in 1979 and is one of China's large state-owned conglomerates. In 2015, the company said that it would invest more than 700 billion yuan (US$112.79) to support the BRI, with investments going to about 300 projects[85].

Private and Overseas Capital

The Chinese government has also been trying to encourage the participation of private capital in the BRI. However, the Maritime Silk Road Bank, set up by the Maritime Silk Road Investment Fund Management Centre (reportedly a private capital company) is the only privately-owned bank in China that make overseas investments on behalf of the country[86].

Of course, BRI projects have not been exclusively financed by Chinese funding sources (even if these may be the largest driving forces). Overseas governments have also raised funds to support or co-finance

Belt and Road related investments, while overseas banks have been keen to capitalize on opportunities arising from BRI related business. HSBC, for instance, states that it, "set a goal of being recognised as the leading bank for BRI in its June 2018 Strategy Update"[87]. Meanwhile, Standard Chartered is amongst global institutions that have signed a Memorandum of Understanding with China Development Bank to facilitate trade and investment related to the BRI. In Kenya, its subsidiary has pledge to support Chinese firms establish and expand their local operations[88].

Multilateral institutions initiated by China

Coinciding with the political upgrading of its economic expansion overseas, China has recently been involved in establishing two new multilateral financial institutions, the Asian Infrastructure Investment Bank and the New Development Bank. While, as multilateral institutions, loans and investments from these banks should not be considered 'Chinese' loans, and while these institutions are not designed to officially favour Chinese investments, they have been expected to be a potentially significant source of financing for BRI projects, and Chinese companies are expected to benefit significantly from contracts related to their lending (on the grounds of experience and competitive pricing).

The Asian Infrastructure Investment Bank (AIIB)

Proposed by Xi Jinping on his state visit to Indonesia in 2013 at the same time that he also set out plans for the 21st Century Maritime Silk Road, the AIIB might be considered especially important to the BRI. Having opened in 2016, with 57 countries joining as founding members and an initial authorized capital of US$100 billion, the AIIB is headquartered in Beijing and can be seen as a China led initiative helping to enhance China's global status and indirectly contribute to the fulfillment of its economic and foreign policy goals. Indeed, although many countries have joined the AIIB as members, China holds by far the largest number of shares (approximately 30%) and controls 26% voting share. The bank has also been actively encouraged to take part in the BRI by Xi Jinping.

By the end of December 2019, the bank had approved loans or financing to 62 projects, at a total value of over US$13 billion. The majority of approved loans have been provided to directly or indirectly finance infrastructure projects in Asia, covering areas such as energy (renewable and non-renewable energies), transport, water, telecommunications and urban and rural development. So far, with 14 loans approved to the country by the end of 2019, (rival) India has been the greatest beneficiary of AIIB financing, receiving more than US$3 billion in loans or almost a quarter of all money lent by the AIIB.

It is worth noting that at its founding in January 2016 the AIIB initially planned to lend US$10 to 15 billion per year for the first five to six years of its operations, but by September 2016 had issued less than $6.4 billion in loans[89], and so far lending has been a lot less than that of similar financial institutions. Between approving its first loan in June 2016 up until September 2018 it agreed to lend just over US$5.2 billion in total. By comparison, the Japanese led ADB lent a two-year total of US$36.6 billion for the years 2016 and 2017[90]. AIIB lending has also been significantly less than other major existing multilateral development banks and only a fraction of the overseas lending of China's policy banks.

Given China's dominant role in the institution, the AIIB has nevertheless sometimes been portrayed as a regional rival to the Japanese led Asia Development Bank (ADB). Major economic rival the United States has also expressed opposition to the institution, viewing it as an attempt to undercut not only the ADB but also the World Bank, and has encouraged its allies to think twice about their participation. China, on the other hand, has been keen to emphasise that the AIIB will complement the work of existing multilateral financial institutions rather than act as a competitor. Indeed, a large number of projects to which the AIIB has provided loans have been co-financed with existing multilateral institutions such as the ADB, World Bank, IFC, EIB. In this sense such loans might not be viewed as competing with the existing institutions but as having a degree of shared interests.

Loans co-financed with other multilateral institutions are also potentially significant for the purposes of holding financial institutions accountable for their lending. In the cases involving co-financing, such loans usually adopt or refer to the exiting institutions' environmental and social impact assessments as their criteria for approving the loan. For loans, where the AIIB is the primary financial institution, the AIIB's own safeguard policies and procedures usually apply, including its Environmental and Social Standards and Environmental and Social Exclusion List.

The New Development Bank (NDB)

The NDB, sometimes referred to as the BRICS bank, is another relatively new multilateral financial institution that can also be considered as furthering China's overseas investment and economic activity, while also supporting domestic development projects. Having opened in 2015 and headquartered in Shanghai, this joint initiative between BRICS countries aims to finance infrastructure projects in the BRICS as well as other emerging economies and developing countries, with priority given to developing renewable energy resources. By the end of December 2019, the bank had approved loans to 49 projects, with a total value of almost US$14 billion. 7 of these projects were categorized as "renewable energy" and a further 5 as "clean energy". The greatest number of projects were categorized as "transportation" projects: 18 in total. Other categories included sustainable development, social infrastructure, and water, sanitation and flood protection. So far, the bank has only provided loans to projects in BRICS countries. Of loans approved at this time, 14 had been awarded to projects in China, 13 to

India, 8 to Russia and 7 to both South Africa and Brazil. Despite until now being limited to BRICs countries, in 2019 bank president, Kundapur Vaman Kamath, stated the intention to expand membership gradually and to mobilise funds for other emerging economies and developing countries[91].

Unlike the AIIB, in terms of governance and management, China does not have such a dominant role in the institution; each of the BRICS country has an equal share and each initially contributed $10 billion. Another distinguishing feature of the NDB is that, according to the NDB's procurement documents, bids for contracts on NDB projects are generally only open to NDB member countries[92] and so currently this only includes BRICS countries. This might be deemed advantageous from China's perspective since it increases the chance of Chinese companies being awarded contracts for development projects financed by the NDB.

Like the AIIB, the NDB has been viewed as a potential rival to the World Bank, IMF and other existing multilateral institutions, meanwhile for some it has also been viewed as offering an alternative to these institutions that have failed to reform and give a greater voice to developing countries. Nevertheless, not only is it much smaller in scale and remit, the bank has also been expected to work with the World Bank and other institutions to co-finance development projects. So far, however, this appears to be much less extensive than AIIB co-financing with other multilateral institutions or fewer details are provided about other lending institutions acting as project co-financees. It is also more common for the NDB's own Environmental and Social Framework (ESF) to be referred to directly as the framework for social and environmental standards and mitigation of adverse impacts than in the case of projects financed by the AIIB.

Social Responsibility and Environmental Protection

Many Chinese banks and institutions have their own social responsibility and environmental protection guidelines for loans and investment. CDB's guidelines, for instance, require projects to comply with local laws and procedures and to report on environmental monitoring efforts (which are not made public) to see if environmental protection requirements have been met. The bank is also a member of the United Nations Global Compact and has pledged to observe the Universal Declaration of Human Rights, the International Covenant on Civil and Political Rights and the International Covenant on Economic, Social and Cultural Rights.

The China Banking Regulatory Commission's (CBRC) Green Credit Guidelines issued in 2012 also apply to the policy and commercial banks and requires all banking institutions to, *"effectively identify, measure, monitor and control environmental and social risks associated with their credit activities, establish environmental and social risk management system, and improve relevant credit policies and process management."* These environmental and social risks:

refer to the hazards and risks on the environment and society that may be brought about by the construction, production and operating activities of banking institutions' clients and key affiliated parties thereof, including environmental and social issues related to energy consumption, pollution, land, health, safety, resettlement of people, ecological protection, climate change, etc. [Article 4][93].

More specifically for overseas investments, Article 21 stipulates that:

Banking institutions shall strengthen the environmental and social risk management for overseas projects to which credit will be granted and make sure project sponsors abide by applicable laws and regulations on environmental protection, land, health, safety, etc. of the country or jurisdiction where the project is located.

Other opinions and guidelines set out by Chinese authorities more recently have also requested that Chinese entities participating in international cooperation abide by relevant local laws and regulations.

Yet, as has been often pointed out, mechanisms for monitoring and enforcing compliance with environmental and social guidelines and regulations remain very weak[94], formal grievance mechanisms are lacking, and public oversight is limited due to lack of disclosure about project information. CDB and Exim bank, for instance, do not disclose basic project information such as environmental and social impact assessments, resettlement plans and monitoring reports[95]. Given some of the risks posed by Chinese loans and investments detailed in this report, the absence of transparent disclosure and grievance mechanisms give reason to be additionally concerned about loans associated with these institutions, and to question the substance of any stated commitment to environmental and social protections.

While multilateral institutions such as the AIIB and NDB, might be easier to monitor, especially where they engage in co-financing agreements and adopt performance standards of other international institutions, this does not mean that these loans will not have a detrimental impact for people and the environment and should not be highly scrutinized by civil society. Indeed, lending by older international institutions such as the World Bank and IMF has also gone towards financing projects that have had destructive environmental and social impacts and contributed to harmful debt distress and poverty through the imposition of structural adjustment programs. This has sometimes encouraged developing countries to look elsewhere for investment and loans in the first place.

Part 4: Hong Kong's role in Chinese overseas investment

Hong Kong has long played a critical role in mainland China's development strategies and facilitated its global economic rise. Despite some greater diversification more recently, the city has continued to be the most important location for China's outbound investment.

Since the beginning of the 1980s, China began to export small sums of capital to Hong Kong for both political and economic reasons, such as to win over the support of Hong Kong capitalists before the handover, as well as to aid Chinese companies to use Hong Kong's experiences to learn Western management, trade and technology skills. Then, in the late 1980s, as mainland China's domestic market reform deepened and central control was gradually relaxed, there was an increasing desire to make money. This period led to a lot of "window companies" of mainland companies being set up in Hong Kong. Corruption, bribery, the misappropriation of public funds and other irregularities were common in this period[96].

In the 1990s, investment continued to pour into Hong Kong as the Chinese government promoted outbound FDI to Hong Kong, and Chinese provincial governments bought shell companies and floats in the Hong Kong stock market[97]. The 1990s also saw the growth of underground banking networks, which have continued to provide a channel for capital flight since then, as wealthy Chinese people seek to move their money overseas[98].

By 1993, China had become the number one investor in Hong Kong, with investment amounting to US$20 billion[99]. Round tripping of investments, whereby Chinese capital is sent to Hong Kong so that it can re-enter China as FDI and receive the preferential treatment afforded to foreign capital, has been a significant phenomenon since this time. Benefiting Chinese capital, this has contributed to the high proportion of investment directed to Hong Kong as a part of China's overseas direct investment figures, and some might describe it as distorting the figures. Estimates continue to place the proportion of Chinese capital involved in roundtripping at about 40%, or between 30-50%, with a large amount of this directed through Hong Kong[100].

Although many of the "window companies" that had been set up in Hong Kong in the early 1990s were hit by the Asian financial crisis in the late 1990s, as mainland China was not heavily hit due to its capital controls, the Central and provincial governments were able to rescue their window companies[101] and they have continued in their role as vehicles to facilitate the growth of mainland Chinese capital.

Chinese capital has benefited from Hong Kong's position as a major international service centre. With Hong Kong's almost unique position under 'one country, two systems' having until recently allowed for greater economic and political freedoms than in the Chinese mainland, it has been an attractive destination for both mainland and international capital, offering a window between the two locations and their doing business with one another. As a result, Hong Kong has become one of the world's leading global financial centres, enhancing opportunities for Chinese businesses, including in their international expansion. Subsequently, Hong Kong has also facilitated the internationalization of the RMB and was the world's largest offshore RMB clearing centre in 2019, sharing about 75% of the worlds RMB payments[102].

The Closer Economic Partnership Arrangement (CEPA), a free trade agreement, which was signed between mainland China and Hong Kong in 2003, represented a further step aimed at increasing trade and business integration. The agreement and its subsequent supplements promote the reduction and elimination of tariffs, the liberalization of trade in services and the promotion of trade and investment facilities, allowing mainland Chinese companies greater access to Hong Kong's financial and business services and Hong Kong companies greater access to the mainland Chinese market.

More recently, Hong Kong has been viewed as a tool in the advancement of the BRI, having been designated a role by China's National Development and Reform Commission (NDRC) in its Vision and Action plan for the BRI. The Plan for this initiative explicitly states that, "We should leverage the unique role of overseas Chinese and the Hong Kong and Macao Special Administrative Regions, and encourage them to participate in and contribute to the Belt and Road initiative"[103]. Echoing the mainland government, the Hong Kong government has similarly stressed the importance of the initiative for the city. This role is one which was then consolidated in December 2017 when Hong Kong Chief Executive Carrie Lam signed an agreement with the NDRC on 'Advancing Hong Kong's Full Participation in and Contribution to the Belt and Road Initiative'. The Hong Kong government has also so far organized two Belt and Road summits in Hong Kong targeting investors, service providers, and project owners and operators promoting business opportunities in relation to the initiative. At the summit, held in September 2017, at which around 3,000 participants were reported to have attended, Secretary for Commerce and Economic Development, Edward Yau, stated that Belt and Road countries would be given priority in the bilateral and plurilateral agreements that Hong Kong is negotiating with other countries and pointed to the recent conclusion of the FTA with ASEAN as an example[104]. He also reported that the Hong Kong government had proposed an agreement with the NDRC (which was subsequently signed in December that year) and which would, "give a very detailed description of areas that Hong Kong is good at, and areas that we believe that Hong Kong can serve the Belt and Road Initiative not just for the country, but also for partners that will be collaborating with the Mainland"[105].

Related to this role for Hong Kong as a part of the BRI, Hong Kong has been integrated into plans for the Greater Bay Area. First conceived of in 2011 in the Action Plan for the Bay Area of the Pearl River Estuary, in March 2017 the plan was officially put forward in the Government Work Report to the National People's Congress. The mainland government's national development plan for the Guangdong-Hong Kong-Macao Greater Bay Area was then unveiled in February 2019[106]. The "Greater Bay Area" aims to integrate nine cities in Guangdong, Hong Kong and Macau. The Chinese government expects the GDP of the area to reach US$4.62 trillion by 2030. According to plans for this Greater Bay Area, which remain vague about detail, Hong Kong will consolidate its status as an international finance, trade, transportation and aviation hub and as an offshore Renminbi business hub. Although first conceived of prior to the BRI, the "Greater Bay Area" has subsequently been described as a "gateway to the BRI".

The following sections provide some more detail concerning the significance of Foreign Direct Investment (FDI) and the Hong Kong stock market in relation to Chinese Overseas Investment, as well as discussing some of the implications of mainland Chinese capital for people in Hong Kong.

Foreign Direct Investment

Hong Kong is the world's third largest host of FDI stock, largely as a result of the role the city plays connecting with mainland China. Mainland China represents both a major source as well as major destination of Hong Kong's total FDI. Part of the reason for this is that, as described previously, Hong Kong has played an important role for roundtrip investments (after coming to Hong Kong, mainland capital is then reinvested back into mainland China) as well as a location for channelling investment to other countries overseas. While there are discrepancies in the statistics concerning the exact figures of FDI involved (perhaps due to differing reporting criteria as well as capital flight), these discrepancies do not detract from the overall picture of the significance of Hong Kong as a recipient and source of mainland FDI.

For many years, Hong Kong has received by far the largest proportion of China's total FDI flows and stock according to mainland official statistics. At the end of 2018, Hong Kong accounted for 55.5% of China's total FDI stock according to these statistics. Meanwhile mainland China is Hong Kong's second largest source of FDI stock, accounting for 26.8% (HK$4,121.6 billion) in 2018, according to Hong Kong Census and Statistics Department data, after the British Virgin Islands which accounted for 31.9% (HK$4909.8 billion). In terms of direct investment inflow, mainland China was the largest source for Hong Kong in 2018, with investment amounting to HK$296.6 billion. In 2018 the mainland's investment ($4,121.6 billion) in Hong Kong mostly went into, "investment and holding, real estate, professional and business services" (78.6%); "banking" (8.8.%); "construction" (5.7%); and "import/export, wholesale and retail trades" (2.6%)[107].

At the same time, in 2018 the mainland was the most important destination for Hong Kong's outbound FDI, receiving 40.6% of the total. This amounted to HK$5,822.8. billion, with a yearly outflow of HK$397 billion and resulted in an income inflow of HK$497.7 billion[108]. Guangdong province received a high proportion of outbound FDI, amounting to 25.9% of Hong Kong's outward direct investment to the mainland. In that year, 80.5% of Hong Kong's total global outward FDI was in investment and holding, real estate and business and services. However, for Hong Kong's investment in the mainland, information and communication services accounted for 30.5%, followed by investment and holding, real estate, professional and business and services (24%), banking (13.3%) and manufacturing (12.1%)[109]. The role of Hong Kong is so significant in this regard that by the end of 2018, of all overseas projects approved in mainland China, 46.3% were tied to Hong Kong interests[110].

Similar investment trends and proportions to those presented here concerning Hong Kong's investments from and in mainland China in 2018 have been observed over several preceding years. Nevertheless, as highlighted in Part One, there has been a small decline in the percentage of China's total global FDI received by Hong Kong in recent years, perhaps indicating a greater diversification in the channels for Chinese FDI. Nevertheless, the decline is still far from representing a situation whereby Hong Kong no longer plays a crucial role for mainland Chinese capital, including in the pursuit of overseas expansion.

Chinese capital and listings in Hong Kong

The Hong Kong stock market has been another extremely important vehicle for Chinese companies and their internationalization, and another reason that Hong Kong has been an important destination for mainland FDI. When the Chinese government was debating opening the mainland Chinese stock market in the late 1980s, it looked towards Hong Kong. Then, with Hong Kong's rapidly growing economy in the 1990s, and with a market capitalization more than eight times China's foreign exchange reserve, Hong Kong provided a good location for mainland Chinese companies to gain access to capital and investors[111]. Today, mainland Chinese companies represent a significant proportion of all companies listed in Hong Kong.

At the end of 2019, there were 1,231 mainland Chinese enterprises listed on the Hong Kong stock market, including private enterprises, "H share" and "Red Chip" companies. Between them, these companies had a total market capitalisation of about US$3.4 trillion, or 73% of the market total[112]. By the end of 2018, nine of the ten largest IPO funds raised by newly Hong Kong listed companies since 1986 were mainland Chinese companies, eight of which were state owned financial institutions and enterprises[113]. Then, in November 2019, Chinese e-commerce giant Alibaba raised US$12.9 billion in its IPO on the Hong Kong stock market, representing the largest IPO since AIA raised almost US18 billion in 2010.

Red Chip companies were (and continue to be) an important type of company listed on the Hong Kong stock market. Red Chip companies are companies that are incorporated outside of mainland China and controlled by mainland government entities, and include major Chinese SOEs, such as China Mobile, Lenovo Group Ltd and COSCO SHIPPING Ports Ltd. At the end of January 2020 there were 173 Red Chip companies listed on the Hong Kong stock exchange, with telecommunications company China Mobile significantly the largest in terms of its market capitalization of approximately 1.3 trillion HKD. Of Red Chip companies that are currently listed, the earliest listing dates are 1972 and 1973 (eight companies were listed). The remainder of the companies were listed from the 1980s onwards. These state-owned red chip companies have been a major form of investment in Hong Kong and in raising capital in Hong Kong to help develop China's economy. Many of these companies have links to high ranking officials in China. The domestic political power structures within the leadership of these companies is not always secure, however, and it has been argued that those controlling some of these companies have been more concerned about personal rather than company interests, leading such companies to concentrate capital in industries that promise quick returns and to engage in speculative activities, contributing to the volatility of property prices and stock prices in Hong Kong[114].

Red chip companies have been seen as advantageous as they do not have to follow the regulations of China Securities Regulatory Commission, which controls new listings and share offerings, and so have the advantage of being able to more easily use funds to acquire overseas investments with than H share companies[115]. COSCO Shipping Ports is an example of a Red Chip company based in Hong Kong that has served this function. It first listed in Hong Kong in 1994 in order to help its parent company, China Cosco Shipping Group, to conduct bank financing. It has bought ports for its parent company in Shanghai, Zhangjiagang, Yantian and Qingdao as well as overseas ports in Greece in 2009 and Turkey in 2015. In 2016, Kelvin Wong Tin-yau, Cosco Shipping Port's executive director and deputy managing director, was reported as having stated that the company expects to acquire more overseas ports in light of the Belt and Road initiative[116].

H-shares are another type of company owned by mainland entities or individuals connected with the Chinese government and traded on the Hong Kong stock market. The H-share was established later than the Red Chip and was first set up by the HKEX in 1993, with Tsingdao Brewery Company the first H-share company. Unlike Red Chip companies that are incorporated in Hong Kong, H share companies are incorporated in mainland China. The H-share index has been outperforming the Red Chip index for many years[117] and a significant number of new companies have listed in recent years. Of a total of 263 companies that were listed on the main board[118] of the Hong Kong stock market at the end of January 2020, approximately 32% had listed since the beginning of 2015. Notable H- share companies include the Bank of China Ltd, China Petroleum and Chemical Corporation and the Industrial and Commercial Bank of China Ltd. With the rise of the mainland stock exchanges, H-share companies have had an advantage in that despite their facing more central control and regulation concerning the raising of new capital, for companies which seek dual listing in the A-share market in mainland China, the Red Chip structure is more complicated than H-shares for raising funds.

The remainder of mainland companies listed on the Hong Kong stock market are Mainland Private Enterprises (MPEs). These companies are described as, "companies that are incorporated outside of the Mainland and are controlled by Mainland individuals"[119]. Following the issuing of the Notification about Issues concerning Overseas Listing of Enterprises by the China Securities Regulatory Commission (CSRC) in July 1999, MPEs have been increasingly allowed to seek listing and funding overseas, as possible candidates for overseas listings were expanded from mostly just SOEs to also include collective and privately owned enterprises[120]. Some backdoor MPE listings occurred much earlier than this. With a comparatively restricted access to funds in the mainland when compared to SOEs, listing in Hong Kong has been an important way for these companies to acquire funds. In 2018, MPEs accounted for 54.8% (HK93 billion) of total post listing funds raised by mainland enterprises in Hong Kong[121].

The Hong Kong stock market looks set to continue to aid in China's global expansion through the increased integration of Hong Kong. The opening of the Hong Kong-Shanghai Stock Connect on 17th November 2014 brought a major change to the Chinese stock market by linking the two stock exchanges and allowing foreign investors outside mainland China access to the mainland Chinese market with fewer restrictions for the first time, and mainland investors to purchase select companies listed in Hong Kong. This was followed by the Shenzhen-Hong Kong Stock Connect which opened in December 2016. Meanwhile, the importance of the Hong Kong stock market for China's outbound investment strategy and the BRI is perhaps also evident. Amongst the Silk Road Fund's initial significant projects, two have involved assisting Chinese SOEs to list on the stock market. It backed the IPO of the investment banking group China International Capital Corporation by purchasing $100 million of shares in 2015. The corporation aims to raise US$50-100 billion for overseas investment including in BRI countries. In 2015, the Silk Road Fund also agreed to purchase US$300 million of shares in the IPO of China Energy Engineering Corporation[122].

What does Chinese capital mean for Hong Kong itself and people in Hong Kong?

The presence of Chinese investment and development plans aimed at driving the closer integration of the SAR with the Chinese mainland can now be felt all over the city. The Greater Bay Area development plans are potentially significant in this regard, given the plan directly promotes greater economic integration between Hong Kong and mainland China[123] but is also given increased weight due to promotion by the central government and integration into its BRI.

In Hong Kong, however, plans for the Greater Bay Area have not been universally popular. Early on it was already receiving criticism from lawmakers claiming that there has been a lack of consultation. While specific plans and implementation details have frequently been vague, due to the way that the Greater Bay Area has been heavily promoted by the mainland government, concerns and criticism have also related to the erosion of Hong Kong autonomy and threats to 'one county, two systems'. The close relationship to Hong Kong's political elites was also highlighted when it came to light that former Hong Kong Chief Executive, Leung Chun-ying, who had begun to heavily promote the BRI, was a director of two companies, Belt and Road Hong Kong Centre Company Limited and the Bay Area Hong Kong Centre Company Limited, that are related to these development plans. Leung has denied that there is a conflict of interest, stating that the companies are non-profit and his role unpaid. Leung became director of the companies on the same day that he stepped down as Chief Executive[124].

One of the most notable specific projects that has been brought under the umbrella of the Greater Bay Area is the Hong Kong-Zhuhai-Macau Bridge (HZMB). At 55km in length, the bridge, which connects the three cities, is the world's longest sea bridge. Construction began on the bridge in 2009 and it was finally completed and inaugurated in 2018 by President Xi Jinping, after having run into numerous controversies during its construction, caused harm to the environment and resulted in the deaths of numerous construction workers. A 2008 LegCo document showed that Hong Kong was expected to shoulder the greatest financial cost for the bridge at 50.2% of the original 31 billion Yuan budget, with the mainland financing 35.1% and Macau 14.7%[125]. However, the financing and budget for the Hong Kong section of the bridge were repeatedly revised and obscured as the project met with several budget overruns, and additional financing from Hong Kong was later sought.

Perhaps more significantly, the unsafe working conditions for those working on the construction of the bridge resulted in a high human cost. With 10 worker deaths and 600 injuries between 2010 and 2018 on the Hong Kong section of the bridge alone (statistics for the mainland section are not known), the bridge earned the nickname 'the bridge of death'. In at least two cases, the companies involved were fined as little as HKD15,000 (less than USD2000) for their negligence leading to each worker death[126].

Meanwhile, safety issues also emerged during construction that could have potentially put the public in jeopardy. In mid-2017, 21 employees from a government contractor were arrested for allegedly faking concrete test reports, which could have undermined the safety of the bridge. Then, in another incident, it was revealed that the Highways Department had failed to disclose the collapse of two seawalls that had taken place two years earlier on reclaimed land, leading questions to be raised about potential cover-ups or illegal land reclamation

It is not only human life that has been threatened or harmed by this project though. The bridge has also been criticised by environmental organisations such as the WWF for destroying marine habitats and leading to a decline in the number of Chinese white dolphins in the northern waters of Lantau since construction began[127].

Although the bridge has been described by the Hong Kong Trade Development Council as being, "of special strategic value in anchoring the Bay Area as the investment services platform for the Belt and Road Initiative by accelerating economic integration and increasing regional competitiveness"[128], the overall benefit to the majority of the people of Hong Kong can be considered highly questionable. In fact, from a Hong Kong perspective the project might be viewed as a white elephant with little prospect of it paying for itself. The bridge is little used. Indeed, a special permit is required to drive across the bridge, with a limit of 10,000 private car permits imposed and only to be issued to those with financial or political contributions on the mainland[129].

The greater costs than benefits to Hong Kong residents of similar megaprojects, such as the US$10 billion highspeed railway linking Hong Kong and Guangzhou in mainland China that opened in 2018, have also led to opposition to these projects. Plans for this project initially met with significant opposition in 2009 to 2010 from the public and civil society organisations who wanted the Legislative Council to reject the bill providing funding to the project. The Anti-Highspeed Railway Movement saw petitions, several protest marches and rallies and a hunger strike, culminating in protesters surrounding the Legislative Council building, in what became dubbed the 'siege of the LegCo' to protest against the bill. Eventually the bill was passed, however, and construction began on the Hong Kong section in January 2010. Ultimately, the project significantly overran its budget and resulted in the eviction of hundreds of villagers from their homes to make way for its construction. This project also later caused significant concern about the erosion of Hong Kong autonomy. This was due to arrangements at the West Kowloon railway station for a joint checkpoint placing part of the station directly under the jurisdiction of Beijing and its law enforcement agencies, despite its location on Hong Kong soil.

Another major area that has been affected by Chinese investment in Hong Kong is housing. In June 2017, it was reported that so far that year mainland Chinese developers has bought up all HK$37 billion of government land sold for residential development[130]. In the second quarter of 2018, Hong Kong received 80% of mainland Chinese property investment[131]. This flood of investment from the mainland has driven up property prices and rents, an issue which has a direct adverse economic impact on many Hong Kong people who are faced with the world's most expensive real estate market.

Interestingly, it is not only ordinary people that have been affected. The increasing presence of mainland capital in the city has also coincided with increasing tensions for Hong Kong local tycoons. In a 2016 interview with the Financial Times, Hong Kong gambling magnate, Lui Che-woo, described how it had becoming increasingly difficult for Hong Kong developers to compete with mainland capital for development sites, with mainland companies able to offer prices that local companies found difficult to match[132]. Meanwhile, there have also been signs of pressure placed on Hong Kong local tycoons to show loyalty to Beijing. During the 2014 Occupy Central Movement, a Xinhua report criticized Hong Kong tycoons for not doing enough to oppose the Movement. The article singles out Li Ka-shing, then Asia's richest man, as well as three other local tycoons. Despite the article subsequently being withdrawn, it was interpreted as a sign that the Chinese central government might be running out of patience with them[133].

An uncertain outlook

In 2019, growing resentment around increased political control by Beijing culminated in the emergence of the anti-extradition bill protest movement and significant political unrest. Interestingly, the movement saw the targeting of mainland Chinese capital in the city by protesters, particularly where the business had expressed support for the government. Thus, a connection was made between mainland China's growing political influence and the activities of mainland Chinese capital in Hong Kong. Although the movement was ultimately successful in halting the extradition bill, its later demands which went far beyond this and included the re-emergence of the call for genuine universal suffrage went unanswered.

The outlook now looks even more dim, leading to questions about the future role of Hong Kong. By early 2020 the movement was already ebbing, however the emergency of the coronavirus pandemic has since provided a pretext for the Hong Kong

Part 5: Strategic Companies and Overseas Investment: COSCO Shipping, CCCC and the Sinopec Group

As outlined in previous sections, the Chinese government has increasingly been promoting and guiding the expansion of investments and related activities by Chinese companies overseas. This section provides a very brief introduction to three companies that have been significant in this regard and which have played an important and strategic role in the BRI. It also provides some examples of these companies' overseas investment activities and associated problems. While the profiles of these companies and their activities are far from complete, it is hoped that they will nevertheless facilitate insight into the nature of Chinese Overseas investments in some of the most strategic industries.

China COSCO Shipping Corporation Limited (COSCO Shipping)

COSCO Shipping is a marine transportation and terminal operation multinational conglomerate. It operates one of the world's largest container fleets, with a 3 million TEU capacity. As of April 2020, the Corporation had invested in 59 terminals, including over 51 container terminals, all over the world[134]. Headquartered in Shanghai, the conglomerate was formed in 2016 as the result of the merger of China Ocean Shipping (Group) Company (COSCO) and China Shipping (Group) Company (China Shipping). COSCO Shipping has numerous subsidiaries, some of which were previously subsidiaries of COSCO or China Shipping, which like their parent also have a major international presence.

COSCO Shipping is one of China's 96 Central SOEs under the State-owned Assets Supervision and Administration Commission of the State Council (SASAC) and therefore of high strategic importance. SASAC is a very powerful commission, which guides and pushes forward the reform and restructuring of SOEs, appoints and removes the top executives of supervised enterprises, and is responsible for working out the state-owned capital operational budget and final account and their implementation[135]. Top executives of COSCO therefore have close ties to the CCP and the company's activities are linked to the pursuit of the goals of the party-state. COSCO Shipping's current Chairman and Party Secretary is Xu Lirong. Xu has a long history working for COSCO.

China COSCO Shipping states that its vision, "is to undertake the mission of globalizing [the] Chinese economy." As a Central SOE, the company's vision is very much in line with that set out by the Chinese Communist Party, and with the BRI setting out a strategy of developing trade and infrastructure corridors from China to Asia, Africa and Europe, the industries that the company is concerned with play a central role in establishing and reinforcing these corridors, while also expanding its business. In May 2019, Chinese media reported that in the past few years COSCO Shipping had invested US$8.12 billion in countries and regions related to the BRI through development of terminals, shipping routes and logistics and was operating 174 container liner routes (1.61 million TEUs) in BRI countries, accounting for 58 percent of COSCO Shipping's total container capacity[136].

It is clear that amongst strategic functions of COSCO Shipping and its subsidiaries is that of expanding trade and infrastructure networks. As well as aiding Chinese companies to invest and access market overseas, another reason that this might be beneficial to China is that it helps guaranteeing transportation and importing of natural resources. This naturally has some geopolitical implications. One example concerns oil. China is the world's largest oil importer and the only major importer of Iranian oil (importing 14.77 million tonnes, or 295,400 barrels per day in 2019)[137]. As a result of their transporting of Iranian oil, some of COSCO Shipping's subsidiaries have been subject to US sanctions. Given the group's major role in the global market, the blacklisting of COSCO Shipping subsidiaries disrupted the global shipping market and sent up the costs of worldwide freight. This might partially explain why these sanctions have not necessarily been applied uniformly, and with developments in US-China trade talks (and not necessarily policy towards Iranian sanctions) changes have been made to the subsidiaries that are blacklisted[138].

COSCO Shipping Ports Limited

COSCO Shipping Ports is an example of one of the notable subsidiaries linked to COSCO Shipping that is also particularly important to the BRI. In recent years (especially since the launch of the BRI) the subsidiary has made significant investments in overseas terminals in strategic locations around the world (see the list below).

COSCO Shipping Ports Limited is a significant subsidiary linked to COSCO Shipping and acts as its port and terminals arm. As of 30 September 2020, COSCO SHIPPING Ports operated and managed 360 berths at 36 ports worldwide, of which 206 were for containers, and had a total annual handling capacity of approximately 115 million TEU[139]. In 2019, it was projected to soon overtake Hutchison Ports to become the second largest ports operator in the world[140].

Founded in 1994 it was previously known as COSCO Pacific Limited. The company is headquartered in Hong Kong and has been listed on the Hong Kong stock market (SEHK:1199) since 2003. It is not immediately directly owned by COSCO Shipping, but is actually the subsidiary of COSCO Shipping Holding's Company Limited (the company owns a 48.84% share), a flagship subsidiary of COSCO Shipping and is headquartered in Tianjin and traded on the Shanghai (SSE:

601919) and Hong Kong stock markets (SEHK: 1919).

COSCO Shipping Ports' Overseas Acquisitions[141]

- **Antwerp Gateway NV** (Belgium): It holds a 20% shareholding.
- **APM Terminals' Zeebrugge** (Belgium): COSCO Shipping Ports finalized a deal to acquire a controlling stake in the container terminal in September 2017. US$42 million acquisition. It has previously bought a 24% share in 2014. Its current shareholding is 85%
- **Bilbao Container terminal** (Spain): A 39.78% share in the Noatum Container terminal .
- **Busan Port Terminal Co., Ltd.** (Korea): COSCO Shipping Ports' current
- shareholding is 4.89%
  COSCO-PSA Terminal Private Limited.
- Singapore: Its current shareholding is 49%.
  CSP Chancay Terminal (Peru): In May 2019, it acquired a 60% equity interest in Port of Chancay representing the company's first greenfield subsidiary in Latin America.
- **Euromax Terminal** (the Netherlands): COSCO Shipping Ports acquired a 35% stake in the Rotterdam for US$145 million.
- **Khalifa Port Container Terminal 2** (Abu Dhabi): COSCO Shipping Ports acquired the for US$700 million. It has a 90% shareholding
- **Kumport Terminal** (Turkey): It holds a 26% shareholding.
- **Port of Pireaus Terminal** (Greece): COSCO Shipping Ports acquired a concession to operate piers 2 and 3 of the container terminal and currently has a 100% shareholding in the terminal according to the company's 2019 annual report. In April 2020, it was announced that management of pier 1 would also be transferred to COSCO Shipping Ports' Greek local subsidiary in Greece, PCT from Pireaus Port Authority (of which COSCO Shipping (Hong Kong) was now the largest shareholder).
- **Suez Canal Container Terminal S.A.E.** (Egypt):
  It has a 20% shareholding.
- **SSA Terminals (Seattle Terminals), LLC** (USA):
  It holds a 13.33% shareholding.
- **Vado reefer and container terminals** (Italy): COSCO Shipping Ports has a 40% shareholding.
- **Valencia terminal** (Spain): In June 2017, COSCO Shipping Ports took over 51 percent of Spanish terminal operator Noatum Port Holdings for US$228 million.

Investment in the Port of Pireaus

Of all its recent investments, COSCO Shipping's subsidiaries' (including COSCO Shipping Ports) acquisition of the Port of Pireaus in Greece is one that has been especially notable. This investment is seen as significant due to its integration into the BRI, China's plans for the port's rapid expansion and China's pursuit of turning it into the major container hub of the Mediterranean. The port, which has served the city of Athens since ancient times, is currently the second largest container port in the Mediterranean and the largest passenger port in Europe.

The port's privatization and acquisition has also been controversial and a cause of high concern from a labour rights perspective.

Although listed on the Athens Stock Exchange since 2003, the Port of Piraeus was previously majority owned by the Greek state. In 2009, COSCO Pacific (now COSCO Shipping Ports) was granted a concession by the Greek government to operate a part of the port (piers 2 and 3 of the container terminal) for 35 years. For this the company had to pay 50 million Euros, pay a sum of revenues each year, make substantial investments in Pier 2 and complete the building of pier 3 so that it could begin operations in 2014. To manage this, COSCO Pacific set up Piraeus Container Terminal SA (PCT) to be its local subsidiary[142].

Following the Greek debt crisis, the EU pushed further privatization in Greece. Despite Syriza's election in 2015 and its previous promise not to further privatise the port, in 2016 this led to a majority share in the Port/Piraeus Port Authority S.A. being sold to COSCO Shipping (Hong Kong) Co., Ltd, a wholly owned subsidiary of COSCO Shipping that describes itself as, "one of the large Chinese enterprises in Hong Kong"[143]. COSCO Shipping (Hong Kong) agreed to pay 368.5 million euros (US$410 million) for the government's 67 percent stake in the port authority. This would involve it initially paying 280.5 million euros for a 51% stake, with the remaining 16% being purchased for 88 million euros after five years, provided that the company invested 350 million euros in the port's expansion and modernization. The breaking of this promise to halt the port's privatization left many in Greece feeling betrayed.

Although carried out through Hong Kong based subsidiaries, investment in the Port of Piraeus seems to have been very important to the Chinese government. Senior Chinese government officials have paid close attention to the acquisition and visited the port on several occasions. In 2019, President Xi Jinping himself visited the port. On his visit, Xi said that the port showed that the BRI was a brilliant reality[144]. Indeed, investments by COSCO subsidiaries in the Port of Piraeus have largely been viewed as successful so far from the Chinese party-state's perspective. Since acquisition, it has become one of the fastest growing container terminals in the world. In its 2019 Annual Report, of terminals where COSCO Shipping Ports has a controlling stake (domestic and overseas), the Port of Piraeus was described as one from which profits were mainly attributable to[145]. The company has also highlighted benefits for the local economy. According to COSCO Shipping Chairman Xu Lirong:

> *We don't simply aim for financial return, but wish to lift the local development through investment...The Port of Piraeus was a small port in the Mediterranean Sea. Since China COSCO Shipping took over operations, the port has become a large port, adding over 8,000 jobs to the local economy. We aim to increase that to 31,000 jobs and also add 0.8 percentage points to Greece's GDP by 2025[146].*

Pireaus (Greece): Photo Globalization Monitor

In November 2019, China and Greece agreed to push ahead with a 600 million euro investment in the port, with the European Investment Bank agreeing to provide a 140 million euro loan to help with the investment plans.

In addition to investment by COSCO Shipping subsidiaries in the Port of Pireaus, in November 2019 OceanRail Logistics S.A., an affiliate of COSCO Shipping Europe, also acquired a 60% stake in Pireaus Europe Asia Rail Logistics S.A. (PEARL S.A.), a Greece based railway operations company. The acquisition would allow OceanRail Logistics S.A. to obtain the railway operation qualification in Europe, thereby consolidating COSCO Shipping's involvement in the China-Europe Land Sea Express Line, a line which effectively connects the 21st Century Maritime Silk Road and the Silk Road Economic Belt[147].

While largely viewed as a success story from China's perspective, local opposition has nevertheless led to some setbacks to COSCO Shipping's expansion into Pireaus, however. In 2019, the Greek government rejected COSCO proposals for a new container terminal following local community opposition[148].

In November 2018, Globalization Monitor visited the Port of Pireaus, and spoke with trade unionists and activists about the acquisition of the port and how labour conditions had been affected since COSCO Pacific had first taken over part of the port's operations in 2009. A lack of discussion and dialogue was one issue that was discussed both concerning the sale of the port —one of the senior trade unionists that we spoke to had only learned of the sale of the port from the Chinese media— and in sharing knowledge of aspects of the port operations. Meanwhile the earlier privatization of part of the port in 2009 had led to a situation where COSCO's permission was needed to make certain changes around the port, for instance

Pireaus (Greece): Photo Globalization Monitor

moving a fence, even though the rest of the port was still owned by the state.

There have also been problems at the port regarding labour rights since COSCO Shipping subsidiaries first became involved in investing in it. Trade unionists reported deteriorating working conditions, inadequate health and safety training procedures resulting in accidents, difficulties negotiating with the management to conclude collective bargaining agreements, as well as the problem of decisions no longer being taken at the port but instead far away in China. Giorgos Gogos, General Secretary of the Greek Dockers Union, expressed the fear that the management were trying to reduce the number of dockworkers they employed in preparation for a situation where the company would make greater use of subcontract and agency workers. In considering the working conditions at Piraeus, it should be noted that the labour law in Greece was also described as having deteriorated following the Greek debts crisis and signing of the Memorandum[149]. This had allowed for a situation in which working conditions had declined despite the company not necessarily having violated the law.

Anti-union activity was another reported problem. According to Anastasia Frantzeskaki from the Greek Federation for Port Employees, some trade union members had faced retaliation or refused promotion while others had been sacked as a result of trade union activity. At the same time, a yellow union had recently been established and was racing with existing unions to sign a collective bargaining agreement.

Although these factors in themselves might not be unique to Chinese investment and are greatly influenced by Greece's own political and economic situation, it was observed that Chinese investment was different compared

Part 5: Strategic Companies and Overseas Investment: COSCO Shipping, CCCC and the Sinopec Group.

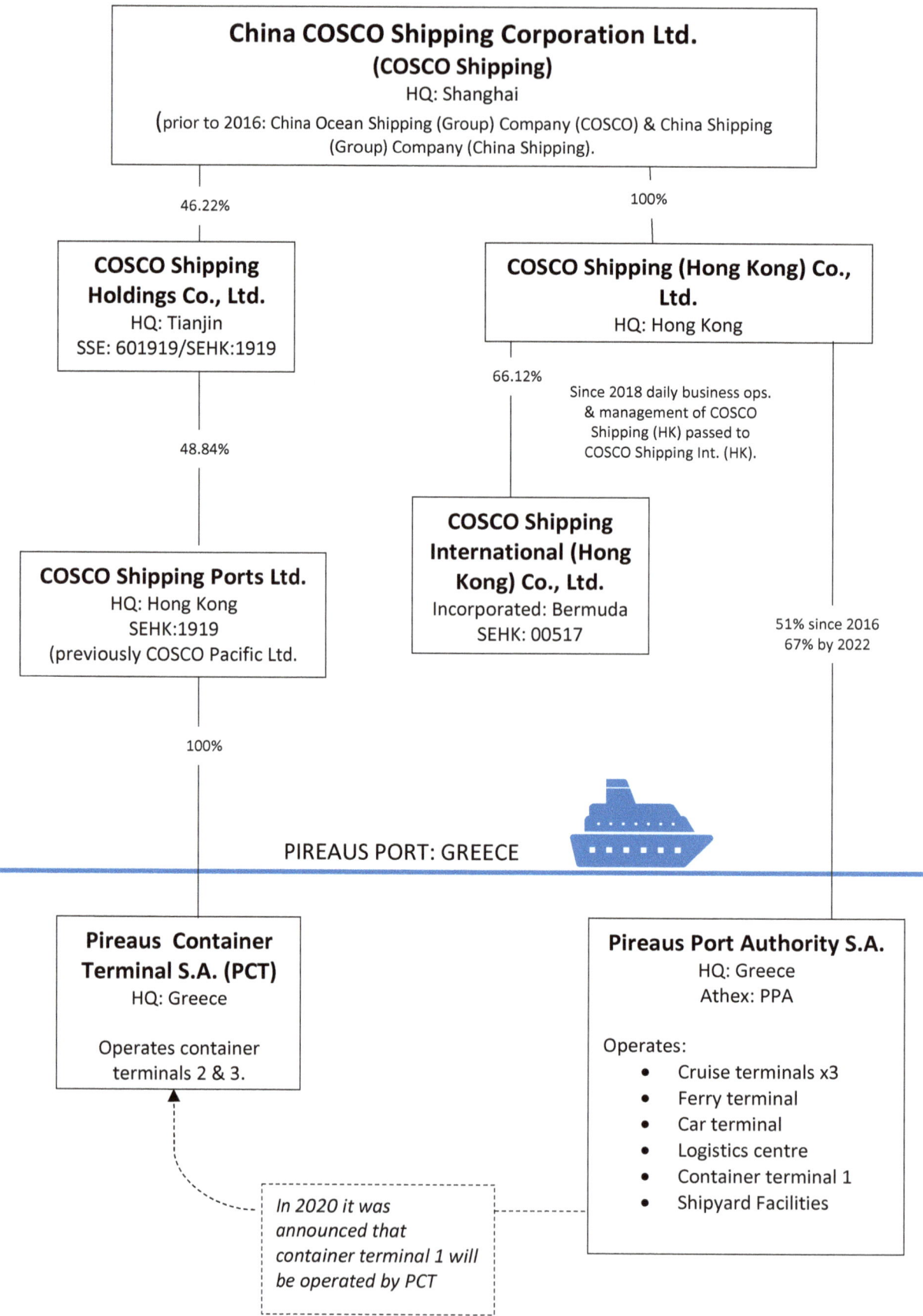

with that from other countries regarding the extent that agreements involved top political officials from both countries. It was also alleged by one interviewee that during an earlier strike COSCO and the Chinese ambassador had together tried (unsuccessfully) to persuade the government to send in special forces to end the strike.

China Communications Construction Company (CCCC)

Headquartered in Beijing, China Communications Construction Company (CCCC) is the largest port construction and design company in China; its major businesses also include dredging, road and bridge construction and design and railway construction[150]. It has more than 60 subsidiaries. At the end of the third quarter of 2018, the total assets of CCCC were worth about 922 billion RMB. From January to September of 2018, CCCC confirmed 1,419 new infrastructure construction contracts—141 of them were overseas projects. It also confirmed 3,272 new infrastructure design contracts during the same period[151].

CCCC was established in 2006, as a result of a merger between China Harbor Engineering (Group) Corporation and China Road & Bridge (Group) Corporation. The origins of these two companies included a series of old state-owned enterprises in related industries[152]. CCCC is one of China' central state-owned enterprises, which means it is directly supervised and governed by the State-owned Assets Supervision and Administration Commission of the State Council (SASAC) and strategically important to the Chinese party-state. CCCC's current chairman of the board is Liu Qitao. Liu is also the party secretary of CCCC[153], and was also elected as a member of the 13th National Committee of the Chinese People's Political Consultative Conference in January 2018 for the term from March 2018 to March 2023.

CCCC is listed on both the Shanghai Stock Exchange (code: 601800)[154] and the Hong Kong Exchange and Clearing (code: 1800)[155]. China Communications Construction Group (Limited) is CCCC's parent company and its top shareholder (with 50.88% of shares). Its second largest shareholder is HKSCC Nominees Limited (27.11%), which is a subsidiary of Hong Kong Exchanges and Clearing Limited[156].

Overseas Projects

As a major construction company, CCCC has been highly involved in a significant number of infrastructure projects overseas, and also described as the BRI's "biggest builder"[157]. To facilitate its overseas activities, the company has established more than 240 branches, research institutes and service hubs in 118 countries and regions. Between 2014 and the end of 2018 it signed overseas contracts worth US$170 billion[158]. In BRI countries it participated in more than 1,600 projects by April 2018[159].

The scale of CCCC's overseas operations and international presence is perhaps worrying however, given the exceptionally high number of corruption and malpractice scandals related to its overseas activities. Indeed, in 2009, it was blacklisted by the World Bank for eight years for alleged fraudulent bidding practices stemming from a highway project in the Philippines[160]. CCCC has denied the allegations. The company or its subsidiaries have also faced allegations related to bribery, corruption or overbilling related to projects in Bangladesh, Malaysia, Tanzania, Sri Lanka Kenya and Equatorial New Guinea amongst others[161]. Having been blacklisted by the World Bank, the extra available financing made available by China Development Bank and EXIM Bank of China as well as commercial lenders for advancing the BRI might be considered especially advantageous to CCCC.

Major Overseas Projects Constructed by CCCC and its Subsidiaries

	Project Name/ Location	Date commenced	Date of Completion	Project Cost	Investment source	Significance	Problems
1	East Coast Rail Link Malaysia	11/2016- contract signed 8/2017- construction began	8/2018- suspended UPDATE as of Nov. 2019- Following negotiation China agreed to reduce the price of the rail link by 34%, the length of the line by 40km, and to increase local participation.	Initial contract- 13.1 billion USD Estimated actual cost- US$20 billion [162]	Initial contract- 85% from Exim Bank, 15% from Islamic bonds by Malaysian investment banks	Flagship BRI project Revitalize the East Coast Region of Malaysia	Corruption, overspending, huge debt to China, hard to profit for Malaysia, most contractors are Chinese companies rather than local companies.
2	Mombasa-Nairobi Standard Gauge Railway, Kenya	7/2012- EPC contract signed 5/2014- financing agreement signed 12/2014- construction began	5/2017- construction completed	US$3.81 billion	90% from Exim Bank, 10% from Kenyan government	Largest infrastructure project in Kenya since independence Replacement of the 100-year old Uganda Railway Further promoting BRI in Africa	No open bidding, huge debt to China, corruption cases, mainly run and staffed by Chinese, racist discrimination against local workers.
3	Hambantota Port (phase 1 and 2) Sri Lanka	1/2008- phase 1 construction began	11/2010- phase 1 completed The end of 2016- phase 2 completed	US$1.761 billion	Phase 1- 85% from Exim Bank, 15% from Sri Lanka Ports Authority Phase 2- 100% from Exim Bank	A potential foothold in the Indian Ocean for China	Not necessary for Sri Lanka, corruption, operating at a loss, huge debt to China, sold to a Chinese company on a 99-year lease to pay off the debt, etc.

4	Gwadar Port (phase 1) Pakistan	3/2002 - phase 1 contract signed	2006 - phase 1 completed	US$248 million	US$198 million provided by China	Near strategic important maritime routes linking the Persian Gulf and Asia Pacific Part of the China–Pakistan Economic Corridor Secure China's energy supply.	Regional instability, Baloch separatism, terrorist attacks, displacement of local communities.
5	Suramadu Bridge Indonesia	8/2003 - construction began	6/2009 - open to the public	US$190 million	90% provided by China through buyer's credit[163]	The longest bridge in Indonesia and the first bridge to cross the Madura Strait Reducing the development gap between Suramadu and Bangkalan The first large-scale transportation infrastructure project China built in Indonesia	Girder collapse accident in 2004

6	Sultan Abdul Halim Muadzam Shah Bridge Malaysia	11/2008 - construction began	3/2014 - officially opened	US$1.45 billion	US$800 million loan from Exim Bank[164]	Longest bridge in Malaysia and in Southeast Asia Key catalyst in the socio-economic development of the Northern Corridor Economic Region of Malaysia.	Ramp collapse accident in 2013, more expensive than initial budget, operating at a loss.[165]
7	Hamad Port (phase 1) Qatar	3/2011 - CCCC subsidiary China Harbour Engineering Company (CHEC) signed the US$880 million contract, construction began afterwards 11/2018 and MOU for Phase 2 was signed between CHEC and Qatar's Ministry and Communication.	2016 - construction completed 12/2016 - port became operational	Total - US$10 billion Contract to CHEC- 1. structural work: US$880 million 2. navy wharf: US$168 million[166]	Qatar government	The largest port in Qatar Important supporting project for the Qatar World Cup in 2022	Not known.

8	Panama Canal 4th bridge	7/2018 CCCC and CHEC jointly won the bid to build the bridge. 5/2019 construction began but soon ran into various problems and construction halted.	Construction is expected to take 54 months and be completed mid 2023	US$1.42 billion	Financing hadn't yet been defined when the contact was awarded but it was hoped that it would be financed locally e.g. local state-owned operator ENA could partly fund it through highway toll charges and the issuing of bonds. When ENA failed to gain a positive evaluation this fell through, the new plan was to obtain a loan to fund construction.	Largest Chinese construction project in Panama	Financing problems, construction delays, corruption probe due to concerns that CCCC and CHEC had been involved in corruption schemes in other countries.[167]
9	Hong Kong-Zhuhai-Macau Bridge	2009/10 construction began. Construction to be carried out by a joint venture consortium led by CCCC. Originally set to open 2016. Repeatedly delayed	Construction completed Feb 2018. Opened October 2018	US$20 billion	Chinese central government, Hong Kong and Macau government to finance 22% of costs, 78% from bank loans, including Bank of China.	The world's longest sea bridge (34 miles). Viewed as a strategic for the 'Bay Area' development plan.	Accused of being a white elephant project, endangering pink dolphins and other marine lives, at least 18 worker deaths and 600 workers injured during the bridge's construction, corruption and safety scandals, lack of financial transparency.

v

60

China Petrochemical Corporation (Sinopec Group)

China Petrochemical Corporation (Chinese: 中国石油化工集团有限公司) or Sinopec Group is a giant petroleum and petrochemical enterprise group. It is the world's largest oil and gas company and ranked second in the Global Fortune 500, with revenues of more than US$430 billion in 2019[168]. In China, people also refer to Sinopec along with CNPC (China National Petroleum Corporation as 'Two Barrels of Oil', as a way to emphasize their dominance and significant influence in China's oil industry.

Like COSCO Shipping and CCCC, the Sinopec Group is a central State-Owned Enterprise (SOE) administered by the State-owned Assets and Administration Commission of the State Council (SASAC). Similarly, the Sinopec Group's leadership are also members of the company's Party Leadership Group, reflecting the control of the Communist Party over the company[169].

According to a document published by China's State Council, Sinopec had 62 subsidiaries when it was first established in 1998[170]. And according to Tianyancha (天眼查), a large data technology service company with a vast repository of Chinese enterprise information, it currently controls or holds shares in at least 65 domestic companies[171]. Among them, China Petroleum & Chemical Corporation (hereinafter referred to as Sinopec Corp) is undoubtedly the most important, since its establishment in 2000 was the result of concentrating the group's most valuable assets. Sinopec Corp is listed in Hong Kong (stock code:00386), New York (stock code: SNP), London (stock code: SNP) and Shanghai (stock code: 600028)[172]. Sinopec Corp itself has multiple subsidiaries and has been active in operations and investment activities overseas.

Another important Sinopec Group subsidiary for overseas investments has been the Sinopec Engineering (Group) Co., Ltd. (hereinafter referred to as SEG). SEG was founded in 2012 after an internal reorganization of Sinopec[173] and listed in Hong Kong the following year[174]. SEG also has subsidiaries or branches in Saudi Arabia, Malaysia, USA, Indonesia, Nigeria, Kazakhstan, Russia, United Arab Emirates and Spain[175].

Overseas Investment

Sinopec has been an active participant in China's 'Going Out' strategy. Given the nature of Sinopec's industry and China's need for natural resources, overseas activities and investments by the company have been of added strategic importance. Indeed, China was already the second largest oil consumer in the world at the beginning of the 21st century, which gave Sinopec's overseas operations the mission of securing China's energy supply. Consequently, the Middle East became the first destination for its overseas investment[176].

In 2001, Sinopec founded its first overseas partner—National Iranian Oil Company (NIOC). Two years later, Sinopec drilled the first oil and gas well in the Kashan Block of Iran[177]. In 2004, Sinopec won a bid to develop a natural gas project in the Sharub Khali Basin of Saudi Arabia. In order to explore and develop this gas field, it formed a joint venture with the stated-owned Saudi Arabian Oil Company (ARAMCO)[178]. In 2009, by acquiring the Swiss company Addax, Sinopec obtained oilfield rights in the Kirkuk region of Iraq[179].

In recent years, Sinopec has continued to expand rapidly overseas, with the BRI having provided further opportunities for Chinese oil companies to continue to invest. By the end of 2017, Sinopec Group had implemented 17 oil and gas cooperation projects in 10 BRI countries[180].

Details of some of the overseas investments that Sinopec Corp is currently operating:

Part 5: Strategic Companies and Overseas Investment: COSCO Shipping, CCCC and the Sinopec Group.

Project	Overview	Major Partner	Amount of Investment
Udmurtia Petroleum Corp (UDM), Russia	Located in the Udmurt Republic, Russia; originally owned by TNK-BP. It was acquired by Russia's Rosneft Oil and Sinopec Corp in 2006 and became a joint-venture between the two. It has 32 oil fields and a daily production capacity of 17,000 metric tons.[181]	PJSC Rosneft Oil Company	Unknown (Rosneft: 51%, Sinopec Corp: 49%)
Caspian Investments Resources Ltd. (CIR), Kazakhstan	Originally owned by Russian company LUKOIL, CIR has 5 oil and gas projects in Kazakhstan. In 2010, one of Sinopec's overseas subsidiaries, Tiptop BVI[182], acquired 50% stakes in CIR with around 1.408 billion USD. Its output in 2013 was approximately 1.02 billion barrels, and the proved total oil and gas reserves were approximately 72.2 million barrels[183]. In 2014, Sinopec Corp agreed to buy the remaining 50% stakes for 1.2 billion USD. However, the international oil price fell sharply soon after the deal, so Sinopec refused to complete the transaction. After negotiating for more than a year, Sinopec eventually bought the remaining 50% stakes for 1.086 billion USD in 2015[184].	None	2010: 1.408 billion USD; 2015: 1.087 billion USD. Since then: unknown.
Mansarovar Energy Colombia Ltd. (Mansarovar), Colombia	Originally owned by Texas-based Omimex Resources. In 2006, Indian SOE ONGC Videsh Limited and Sinopec bought Omimex de Colombia together for 850 million USD and formed the 50/50 joint-venture[185]. In 2013, Sinopec bought a 50% stake in Mansarovar from its parent company for 428 million USD that included the takeover of a loan of 348 million USD from Mansarovar's shareholders[186]. In 2017, Mansarovar produced 11,156,658 barrels of oil[187].	ONGC Videsh Limited	2006: 850 million USD (ONGC: 50%, Sinopec Corp: 50%). Since then: unknown.
Yanbu ARAMCO Sinopec Refining Company (YASREF), Saudi Arabia	This is Sinopec's first overseas refining and chemical project. Agreement signed in 2012, then in 2014 Sinopec Corp bought a Dutch company called COOP from Sinopec for 562 million USD and indirectly obtained the 37.5% stakes of YASREF[188]. The project went into test operation in April 2015, and started production in January 2016[189]. It can process 400,000 barrels of crude oil per day to produce premium transportation fuels and other high-value refined products[190].	ARAMCO	2012: 8.6 Billion USD (ARAMCO: 62.5%, Sinopec Corp: 37.5%)
Repsol Sinopec Brasil, Brazil	Repsol S.A. is an energy company based in Spain. In 2010, Sinopec Corp bought 40% of its Brazilian subsidiarity for 7.1 billion USD and turned it into a joint-venture[191]. In 2018, the joint-venture's net daily oil production was 48,391 barrels[192].	Repsol S.A.	2010: 7.1 billion USD. Since then: unknown.
Block 18, Angola	In 2010, Sinopec Corp acquired 55% stakes of Sonangol Sinopec International (SSI), which has a 50% stake in Block 18, in Angola's deep waters. The remaining 45% is controlled by a mysterious joint venture registered in Hong Kong[193][194].	China Sonangol International Holding Limited (安中国际石油控股有限公司)	2.457 billion USD

Details of some of the overseas projects that SEG has been involved in:

Project	Overview	Major Partner	Amount of Investment
Phase II of Abadan Refinery Upgrading project, Iran	Commissioned in 1912, Abadan refinery is the longest-running Iranian crude refinery and once the largest oil refinery in the world. SEG won the EPC (engineering, procurement and construction) contract in 2017, which is expected to be completed in four years[195]. Financing for the project is coming from China's state-owned export credit insurance agency Sinosure[196].	National Iranian Oil Engineering and Construction Company[197]	6.858 billion RMB [198]
Al-Zour Refinery Project, Kuwait	In 2015, a consortium formed by SEG, Spanish Técnicas Reunidas S.A. and Korean Hanwha Engineering & Construction won the EPCC (engineering, procurement, construction and commissioning) contract from Kuwait National Petroleum Company (KNPC). The refinery is expected to have the largest capacity in the Middle East when completed[199].	Técnicas Reunidas S.A., Hanwha Engineering &Construction, KNPC	Approximately 4.24 billion USD (SEG: 40%)[200]
RAPID Oil Refining Project, Malaysia	In 2014, SEG won the EPCC contract for the Refinery & Petrochemical Integrated Development (RAPID) complex in Pengerang, Johor State[201]. The project has already begun operation.	Petroliam Nasional Berhad (PETRONAS)	1.329 billion USD[202]

Other Overseas Investment

In addition to the investments and projects mentioned above, Sinopec Group and its subsidiaries have many other overseas investments. Some examples include:

Project	Overview	Investment amount
OXY Argentina	In 2010, Sinopec acquired US oil firm Occidental Petroleum (OXY)'s Argentine subsidiary and its affiliates. By the end of 2009, this company's total proven and probable reserves (2P) were 393 million barrels of oil equivalent.[203]	2.45 billion USD[204]
Junin 1 and Junin 8 Blocks, Venezuela	Contract was signed in 2010 as part of China's 40 billion USD investments to Venezuela's oil industry[205].	Unknown
Apache Corporation, Egypt	In 2013, Sinopec bought a 33% of American company Apache Corporation's assets in Egypt[206].	3.1 billion USD[207]
Galp Energia Brasil, S.A.	In 2012, Sinopec bought a 30% stake in Portuguese company Galp Energia, SGPS, S.A.'s Brazilian subsidiary[208].	5.156 billion USD[209]
OML138, Nigeria	In 2012, Sinopec bought a 20% stake in OML138 from French company Total S.A[210].	2.46 billion USD[211]
Talisman Sinopec Energy UK Limited	In 2012, Sinopec bought a 49% stake in Canadian company Talisman's UK subsidiary[212].	1.5 billion USD[213]
Addax Petroleum	In 2009, Sinopec fully acquired this Swiss company[214].	7.2 billion USD[215]

Damaging consequences

As a major oil conglomerate, the Sinopec Group's activities pose significant environmental risks. The company has been frequently criticized for causing damage to the environment. In the mid-2000s, Sinopec was accused of dynamiting and polluting Loango National Park and destroying the forest while prospecting for oil in Gabon, resulting in the Gabon government ordering Sinopec to stop its activities[216][217]. The company (along with other Chinese oil companies) has also been criticised for lagging behind Western counterparts in the approaches adopted to environmental and social standards concerning their FDI[218]. In Angola, for instance, Sinopec does not routinely conduct environmental and social impact assessments, whereas British Petroleum and Chevron do[219]. In 2012, Sinopec announced that it was issuing the first white paper on environmental protection by a Chinese company and stated commitment to clean production, raising resource efficiency, developing green energy and providing sufficient funds for environmental protection[220]. Nevertheless, the company continues to engage in activities that have very harmful effects on people and the environment.

In South Sudan, where Sinopec is part of Dar Petroleum Operating Co., [221]one of two major consortiums that operate there, the oil industry has caused severe environmental damage by leaving hundreds of open waste pits and contaminating the soil and water with toxic chemicals and heavy metals. This is believed to have had significant health impacts on residents and led to birth defects. The government and oil consortiums have been accused of trying to silence those who have tried to expose the problem. Several studies since 2013 have nevertheless confirmed the severe oil pollution (including pollutants that have potentially serious health effects), including a 2018 report commissioned by Dar Petroleum Operating Co. itself, which found extremely high levels of hydrocarbons, 650 waste pits with arsenic and lead contaminated water and ponds gilled with millions of litres of water contaminated with drilling chemicals[222]. According to an Associated Press report, in December 2018 South Sudan's government instructed Dar Petroleum Operating Co., to move ahead with a proposed clean-up, but by early 2020 two people with close knowledge of the situation were claiming that the consortium had never acted[223].

Workers for Sinopec group subsidiaries have also sometimes faced lax safety standards and violations of their rights. In 2013, Sinopec subsidiary SSEC Canada Ltd. was ordered to pay $1.5 million workplace safety fine by an Alberta court, following the deaths of two temporary Chinese workers in 2007 at an oil sands construction site when a tank roof collapsed. Five other workers were injured, two seriously, in the incident. The order came following long legal proceedings in which SSEC Canada had eventually pleaded guilty to three charges under Alberta's Occupational Health and Safety Act. The fine was the largest penalty the Alberta government had ever imposed on a single defendant, although the local labour federation argued it was insufficient for a global giant such as Sinopec[224]. During the investigation following the workers' deaths, the Alberta government is also reported to have found that Chinese workers were not paid for several months of their employment by their employer SSEC, although Canadian Natural Resources Ltd. (the company that had contracted the construction to SSEC), had eventually paid the workers or their families. SSEC had brought 132 temporary workers from China to work on the construction site[225].

Corruption has been another major issue for the Sinopec Group both domestically and internationally. In 2015, China's anti-corruption watchdog reported that it had uncovered evidence of graft, with some executives suspected of corruption in multiple project areas, including in overseas investments[226]. Former Sinopec Group president, Wang Tianpu, was jailed for 15 and a half years for graft by a Chinese court in 2017. Specifically related to overseas investment, in August 2017, the US Department of Justice and the Securities and Exchange Commission started an investigation into Sinopec over suspected US$100 million of bribes paid to Nigerian officials to settle a business dispute. Earlier that year, the corporation had already been required to pay 31 million Swiss francs (about US$32 million) after the company admitted organizational deficiencies[227]. According to the Swiss probe, the company and two executives were suspected of bribing foreign officials[228]. By the end of 2017, it was reported that Sinopec was trying to sell off its Nigerian and Gabonese businesses that had been acquired through its purchase of Swiss company Addax Petroleum in 2009[229].

Part 6: China in Africa

The PRC has long standing engagement with Africa. From the 1950s until reform, it provided assistance to Africa's liberation movements and aid to more than 800 projects, including in agriculture, fisheries, energy, infrastructure, water conservation and power generation. In the 1980s engagement then became based around the idea of 'third world' solidarity[230]. China has, however, also taken a growing interest in Africa in relation to its resources, markets and diplomacy, particularly following the 1990s when the need for new sources of energy and natural resources to support rapid economic growth as a result of reform became increasingly apparent. This need for raw resources is in many ways similar to reasons leading to Europe's scramble for Africa in the late nineteenth century as it went through industrialization.

In 2000 the Forum on China-Africa Cooperation (FOCAC) was established as a ministerial conference held every three years involving China and the 50 African nations with which it had diplomatic relations to enhance cooperation. Each forum develops an action plan for the years that follow. The forum often sees large amounts of loans and aid offered to African countries by China.

Trade and investment have grown substantially. By the mid-2000s, over 800 companies were trading in 49 African countries [231] and by 2010 China had surpassed the US to become Africa's largest trading partner. By 2014 trade with Africa had surpassed US$174 billion, having grown from US$1.3 billion in 1992[232]. According to one report, by 2019 there were 10,000 Chinese companies operating in Africa[233]. Meanwhile, in terms of FDI, while the World Investment Report found a three-fold increase in Chinese FDI stock in Africa between 2009 and 2014, it still ranked behind that from the UK, US and France[234]. China has also been involved in financing and constructing a significant number of infrastructure projects in various countries throughout Africa.

On one hand China's involvement in Africa has been presented as helping to boost the economies and development of African countries, however serious concerns have been raised over whether this comes at too high a price. China's lack of commitment to human rights and press freedom, support for corrupt leaders of undemocratic regimes, labour rights violations and the lack of creation of local jobs have all been criticised[235].

Where and in what is China investing?

A lot of China's investment in Africa has gone into energy, mining, infrastructure construction and manufacturing. Access to resources has been one important driving factor. Exports to China were still mostly in the form of natural resources as of 2015, with crude oil, iron ore, diamonds and agricultural products comprising 56.5% of imports from Africa in the first three quarters of 2015[236].

At the same time, China has also been keen to shift its labour intensive industries to Africa as well as to export its excess capacity. Development of infrastructure has been one means to achieve this, both directly through construction and indirectly by providing enhanced infrastructure to support exports and manufacturing. China had therefore already been investing significantly in infrastructure long before the BRI was announced. According to a recent Deloitte report, by 2018 China was financing one in five infrastructure projects in Africa and constructing one in three[237]. As well as constructing ports, roads and railways, Chinese companies have also been contracted for multiple construction projects to develop power generation plants, hospitals, schools and agriculture.

Chinese companies have also increasingly been setting up factories and investing in manufacturing in African countries. One major example involves investment in shoe manufacturing in Ethiopia, where the Huajian Group, one of the world's largest manufacturers of women's shoes, has been operating since 2011 in the country's Eastern Industrial Zone. Having opened a second factory in its own industrial park just outside of Addis Ababa in 2016, Huajian has continued to expand its investments. In 2019, the company signed an agreement to operate Ethiopia's Jimma Industrial Park, promising to invest US$100 million to construct shoe manufacturing and coffee processing plants and to encourage other Chinese companies to set up in the industrial park[238]. Another example involves automobile manufacturing in South Africa. In 2014, Chinese automaker FAW opened a R600 million factory in the Coega Industrial Development Zone in South Africa. Then two years later, in 2016, another Chinese manufacturer, the Beijing Automobile International Corporation (BAIC) announced that it planned to invest almost US$800m to set up a factory in the same zone. The investment represented the biggest investment in vehicle production in South Africa in 40 years[239]. The factory opened in 2018 and aims to have the capacity to build more than 100,000 vehicles per year by 2027.

Despite growth in investment in manufacturing, however, recent research has found that Southeast Asian countries, partially due to proximity, are often a preferred destination over Africa for many light manufacturers considering overseas investment[240].

One notable strategy for investment (both resource seeking and for manufacturing) in Africa promoted by the Chinese government has been investment in Special Economic Trade Zones (SEZs) and industrial parks. With SEZs having played an important role in China's own economic 'miracle', following China's 'going out' strategy, China has also promoted the establishment of overseas industrial and trade zones. Africa was a key target for the establishment of these zones. Presented as a way to boost the economic development in the countries concerned, these zones would also increase demand for Chinese machinery, improve infrastructure thereby benefiting trade and exports, and provide tax and other incentives for Chinese companies to invest. Since 2006, eight SEZs were approved in six African countries – Nigeria (2 zones), Zambia (2 zones), Ethiopia, Algeria, Egypt and Mauritius. Unlike other SEZs where the governments of affected zones established the zones of their own initiative, Chinese SEZs have been described as a "re-territorialisation of the Chinese state abroad" and are initiated by the Chinese government (through MOFCOM) and operated by the developers or managers of the zones that might include SOEs, private enterprises or public organisations[241], with the aim of boosting Chinese economic development. Meanwhile, the establishment of such zones overseas has also been described as "building a nest to accommodate the Phoenix" (zhu chao yin feng), in other words to accommodate China without much regard for the needs of the host country[242]. Indeed, the terminology used to describe these overseas zones has changed in many recent Chinese publications to distinguish between the SEZs in China and those overseas, indicating how the model proposed in Africa did not replicate the 'Chinese model'[243].

While still promoted both in Africa and other locations subsequently included along the New Silk Road[244], the zones in Africa have experienced different (and often limited) degrees of success. By 2015, the Suez Canal zone in Egypt was described as the only zone that was fully operational. The Jinfei SEZ in Mauritius, having experienced continuous setbacks, had been unsuccessful in attracting Chinese companies and stood largely empty[245][246]. The Jiangling SEZ in Algeria had also failed, something which has been partially attributed to the divergence in visions by the Chinese side that wished the zone to be an enclave for Chinese companies, and the Algerian government that wanted it to benefit Algerian companies and Algerian development[247].

A large amount of Chinese investment in Africa is held by a relatively small number of large SOEs. In 2013 about 100 large Chinese state owned or controlled companies accounted for about 55% of the total Chinese investment in the continent[248]. Nevertheless, although the amounts invested are often lower, the number of private companies investing in the continent have also been growing. Of 10,000 Chinese companies currently operating in Africa, McKinsey estimates that 90% of them have private ownership[249]. Moreover, accompanying larger investments (state and private) and the growth of Chinese overseas networks, hundreds of thousands of individual entrepreneurs from China have also been estimated to have gone to Africa to try to make their fortune.

Belt and Road Initiative

As in Asia, the launch of the BRI has meant a heightened focus on investments and infrastructure construction involving Chinese capital and corporations. Strategically situated on the BRI corridor, east African countries, especially those close to the horn of Africa, have initially been the main focus of the BRI. Kenya and Ethiopia were among 30 countries to sign BRI cooperation agreements at the first Belt and Road Forum held in Beijing in 2017. However, since then the BRI has been further pushed throughout the continent. By the end of September 2019, 40 out of 55 African states had signed BRI Memorandum of Understanding with China for the financing of infrastructure, such as highways, airports and railways[250]. While the extent to which some of these agreements will be implemented is yet to be seen, that so many countries have signed on to the initiative might be considered testament to China's growing influence.

Selected Investment Examples by Country

Chad

- Chad is an important source of oil for China. Chad has had a closer relationship with China since 2006 when the country transferred diplomatic ties from Taiwan to China. In 2007 China then bought the rights to a large oil exploration zone. A large proportion of the Chinese royalties for oil have been invested in arms and training the Chadian army. The World Bank group had also previously provided loans to Chad on condition that oil royalties be used for health and education, but it withdrew funding in 2008 and requested Chad pay the loans back in response to the loans being used for defence spending. As a result of oil royalties Chad has been able to build up its military and has used it against Islamist rebels, regaining Western support (Besliu 2013). In 2014 Chad fined Chinese oil company CNPC's local subsidiary in Chad US$1.2 billion for repeatedly violating environmental standards[251].

- China has also been involved in infrastructure projects in Chad including roads, railroads, hospitals.

- In July 2019 Chad signed a US$216 million agreement for a telecom infrastructure modernization with the Chinese government[252].

Djibouti

- In 2013, China Merchants Port Holdings, a Hong Kong based subsidiary of the Chinese state-owned China Merchants Group acquired a 23.5% stake in the Doraleh Container Terminal. In 2015 construction of the Doraleh Mulit-purpose Port (which opened in mid-2017) began and was jointly financed by China Merchant Holdings International (another subsidiary of the China Merchants Group) and the Djibouti Port and Free Zones Authority. The port is currently a source of dispute and legal action; in November 2018, Dubai based port operator DP world sued China Merchants in Hong Kong for bypassing a concession agreement it had with Djibouti to acquire a stake in the terminal[253].

- Infrastructure networks connecting the port to neighbouring Ethiopia were also being constructed with Chinese financing at around the same time. The Ethio-Djibouti railway, which runs for 750km and also began operations in 2017, for instance, was constructed by China Railway Group Ltd. and China Civil Engineering Construction Corporation and financed by Exim Bank[254].

- The first phase of the Djibouti International Free Trade Zone was launched in July 2018 with the help of China. The zone, which is Africa's largest free trade zone is a US$3.5 billion project, spanning 4,800 hectares. The zone will be managed by Djibouti along with three Chinese companies: China Merchants Group, Dalian Port Authority, and IZP[255].

- In 2016, China began construction of its first overseas military base in the country. Djibouti is a significant location as it already also hosts America's largest military base in Africa and is strategically located between the Red Sea and Gulf of Aden, providing a gateway to the Suez Canal. According to state media Xinhua, in addition to escorting peacekeeping and humanitarian aid, the base, "will also be conducive to overseas tasks including military cooperation, joint exercises, evacuating and protecting overseas Chinese and emergency rescue, as well as jointly maintaining security of international strategic seaways"[256].

Egypt

- China is the largest international investor in the Suez Canal corridor, a major transit point between the Indian Ocean and the Mediterranean Sea, and previously China's primary access point to Europe. China has been interested in upgrading the port of Port Said and the capacity of the canal[257]. In 2008 COSCO Pacific invested US$185.6 million in a joint venture to operate and manage the Suez Canal Container Terminal. China Harbour Engineering Company invested US$219 million to construct a 1200 metre quay in this port's second development stage which has been operating since 2012[258].

- China Railway Construction Company has also been involved in the construction of a 70km railway from Cairo. The contract worth US600 million was awarded to the company in 2015.

- Having previously agreed US$7 billion dollars in investments in Egypt, in 2019 China agreed to increase this amount to US$15 billion.

- In January 2019, Egypt signed a US$1.2 billion loan agreement with the Export-Import Bank of China to finance an electric railway project.

Ghana

- The Atuabo Freeport: a new port will be built at Atuabo for US$600 million by Chinese companies[259]. In 2015, CHEC won the contract to construct the port and construction was expected to be completed within 25 months.

- The Atuabo Gas Processing Plant, built by SINOPEC petroleum and financed by Chinese banks, began production in 2015[260].
-
  In 2018, China and Ghana signed a MOU, part of which included Beijing providing financing for US$2 billion of infrastructure (rail, road, bridges) in exchange for access to 5% of Ghana's bauxite (a mineral used to produce aluminium) reserves. As part of the deal Beijing also agreed to fund 100 vehicles for the Ghana police service, offered a 300 million yuan grant and to write off 250 million yuan of debt. The agreement has received a lot of criticism due to the environmental impact of the bauxite mine and future debt risks and reliance on China for Ghana[261].

Kenya

- US$3.6 billion in credit was agreed at the first BRI Forum for the extension of the Naivasha-Kisumu Standard Gauge Railway (SGR) line. It was later planned for the railway to extend from Kenya's coast to Uganda. But in 2019 construction halted when China suddenly decided to withhold US$4.9 billion of financing needed to complete it. It has been speculated that high profile concern over Kenya's potential for unsustainable debt and China's recent signaling that it would exert tighter oversight over its overseas projects may have triggered the decision to halt the financing[262].

- In 2014 China Communications Construction Company signed a US$479 million deal to build three berths at the Port of Lamu. Two berths were set to handle cargo, while the third would be for crude oil export. The port was scheduled to receive its first ship in late 2019 and for the other two berths to open in 2020.

- Kenya is China's largest trading partner in Africa, with bilateral trade amounting to US$5.3 billion in 2018.

Mozambique

- For the period 2013 to 2015, the Mozambican government requested funding from China for 11 infrastructure projects with an overall budget of US$1.4 billion. This included a loan for the reconstruction of the fishing port of Beira.

- China has been involved in construction projects for the Maputo International Airport, Zimpeto National Stadium, Maputo Ring Road, the Presidency building, rebuilding National Road 6 between Beira and Machipanda[263], and the Maputo-Katembe bridge (opened - 2018).
The Agricultural Testing and Development Centre sponsored by the Chinese Ministry of Commerce opened in Mozambique in 2012 and hosts representatives from Chinese and Mozambican ministries, research agronomists and Chinese SOEs. It also operates a commercial farm on government concession land.

- While officially considered 'development assistance', Chinese Ministry of Commerce directives are reported to have emphasized profitability as the goal of the project[264].

Nigeria

- The Lekki deep-sea port, located in the Lagos Free Trade Zone, is being built by China Harbour Engineering Company Limited (CHEC), the engineering and construction arm of CCCC. The agreement was first formally signed by CHEC and the Lekki Port Company in 2012, with the value of the contract worth around US$679 million. However, it suffered years of delays and it was not until 2019 that a financing agreement was signed with China Development Bank to provide the Singapore based Tolaran Group and CHEC with funding to build the port. In May 2020, it was reported that the project had received over US$221 million equity funding from CHEC[265]. Upon completion, which is expected to be in 2022, it was agreed that CHEC will operate the port under a 45-year concession[266].

- The Ogun-Guangdong Free Trade Zone is located in Ogun State close to Lagos and was one of the first eight overseas free trade zones approved by the Chinese government. According to the Chinese government, the start-up phase of the zone is 2.24 square kilometers and has a cumulative investment of US$325.3 million. In July 2018, it had 50 registered enterprises of which 26 had been completed and put into operation[267].

South Africa

- China Development Bank (CDB) and the Industrial and Commercial Bank of China has loaned millions of dollars to state-owned power company Eskom. The proposed loans have been met with criticisms and protests from civil society activists, concerned about the implications that loan repayment will have on tariffs. In 2019 CDB was unable to disburse funds to Eskom on time reportedly due to central bank exchange control requirements. This created further liquidity problems for the company that was already facing severe difficulties[268].

- South Africa is also a member of the New Development Bank and recipient of loans. Again, concern has been raised by civil society about a lack of transparency and currency risks due to the majority of loans being dollar denominated. A US$200 million loan from the NDB to logistics company Transnet for the rehabilitation of Durban port's container terminals has been criticized for lack of due diligence[269].

- In July 2018 President Xi Jinping pledged more than US$14.7 billion investment in South Africa. This included further loans to Eskom and Transnet as well as planned investments in electronics firm Hisense and a metallurgic complex in Limpopo province[270].

Tanzania

- When plans for Tanzania's Bagamoyo port were agreed with China in 2013, it was to become Africa's largest port and would connect with several East African countries. It was to be funded by China Merchants Holdings, which would also construct railways and a special economic zone, and Oman's State Government Reserve Fund. China secured an investment of US$10 billion in 2015 for the port[271]. However, the port plans were seemingly put on hold in 2016 due, "to austerity measures introduced in Tanzania in order to reduce the widening budget deficit"[272]. Negotiations continued to stall and in June 2019 Tanzania suspended the project indefinitely and unhappy with the conditions that the Chinese company was offering, issued an ultimatum to China Merchants Holdings that it should accept Tanzania's terms or leave. Tanzania's government rejected the Chinese company's demand for a 99-year lease and instead offered a lease of 33 years, denied the company the tax-free status and special water and electricity rates it requested, denied China Merchants the ability to open and operate businesses within the port without receiving government approval and stated that the country would be free to develop other ports to compete with Bagamoyo. The government stated that if China Merchants was to agree to these terms it could proceed with the port project[273].

- China is involved in plans to revitalize the TAZARA Tanzania-Zimbabwe railway that was first build in the 1970s with China's help. The railway was the largest single foreign aid project that China was involved in at that time. However, it has faced continuous operational difficulties and has relied on continued assistance from China, Europe and the US. In 2011 China cancelled half the debts (from an interest free loan) that it was owed by the railway and has since injected additional money and equipment into supporting the railway[274].

Zambia

- The Chambishi copper mine was the first overseas mine to be acquired by a Chinese SOE[275]. In 2018, NFC Africa, a company that is majority owned by China Non-ferrous Metals Company Limited, launched a new US$832 million dollar mine. This is the third mine mined by NFC Africa in Chambishi[276].

- The Zambia- China Economic Cooperation Zone was the first overseas economic trade and cooperation zone to be established in Africa. Established in 2007 and located in Zambia's copper belt, it consists of two multi-facility zone – a 11.58 square kilometre zone in Chambishi focusing on the development of the nonferrous metal industry, and a 5.7 square kilometer zone in Lusaka East focusing on commercial enterprises and logistics.

- The Kafue Gorge hydropower plant is being built by Sinohydro. Construction began in 2015, with 85% of the financing reportedly coming from China's Exim bank and the Industrial and Commerical Bank of China. The government of Zambia was would provide the remainder of the funding. In 2019, however, it was reported that Sinohydro had halted construction after the Sinohydro's services were reportedly not paid for[277].

- In the first half of 2019, China injected US$260 million of direct investment into different sectors of Zambia's economy[278].

- China has been keen for the Tazara railway (see section on Tanzania) to play a role in Zambia's development[279].

- Zambia is China's second largest trading partner in Africa. In 2018 bilateral trade amounted to more than US$5 billion (over US$4 billion in exports to China).

Case study: Mombasa-Nairobi Standard Gauge Railway (Kenya)

Nairobi is Kenya's capital and largest city, while Mombasa is its second-largest city and home to the country's only large seaport, the Kilindini Harbour. An old railway line connecting the two cities was part of the Uganda Railway built by the British colonizers more than one hundred years ago and did not meet modern needs——the trip could take longer than 24 hours[280].

In the early 2000s, the East African Community (EAC) proposed rejuvenating the existing railways serving Tanzania, Kenya, Uganda and extending them initially to Rwanda and Burundi and eventually, to South Sudan, Ethiopia and beyond.[281] A new railway line between Mombasa and Nairobi was also included in this so-called East African Railway Master Plan.

The plan provided an opportunity for Chinese investment and has been viewed as a project of strategic significance by Chinese officials. In August 2009, the Kenyan government and the China Road & Bridge Corporation (CRBC) signed a memorandum of understanding and cooperation concerning the Mombasa-Nairobi Standard Gauge Railway (SGR). In January 2011, CRBC completed a project feasibility study report and in July 2012 an EPC (Engineering, Procurement and Construction) contract for the project was signed[282]. In May 2014, Chinese Prime Minister Li Keqiang and Kenyan President Uhuru Kenyatta then signed the financing agreement to fund the SGR project. According to the Forum on China-Africa Cooperation, the total cost was 3.81 billion USD, and 90% of the financing was to be provided by the Export-Import Bank of China[283]. On December 12, 2014, construction officially started and in May 2017 it was completed and trial operations began[284]. China's State councilor Wang Yong attended the opening ceremony. He said that the SGR was a significant early achievement of the BRI and would play an important role in promoting BRI into the hinterland of Africa[285].

Clearly important for China, what have the implications of this project been for Kenya? The railway has been beneficial in the way that it has reduced the travel time from Mombasa to Nairobi to only about 5 hours, and early indications have suggested that the line has been quite popular, with the train carrying 2 million riders in the first 17 months of operation[286]. Nevertheless, there have also been scandals and criticisms.

Opponents have argued that the cost of the SGR was too expensive and that the huge debt will become a burden for Kenya. They have also asserted that political elites must have been bribed and that this is the reason why the construction was not bid on openly[287].

Another Chinese company, Third Railway and Design Institute Group Corporation (TSDI), won the SGR tender for the, "supervision of construction, procurement and installation of facilities, locomotives and rolling stock" in 2014. Critics argued that this company is closely linked with CRBC. For example, both of their parent companies are controlled by SASAC. An Italian company also protested that it was ruthlessly locked out of this tender bidding process by top insiders[288].

Allegations of corruption might not all be completely groundless. In November 2018, prosecutors in Kenya charged three senior CRBC employees with trying to bribe detectives investigating fraud involving ticket sales. The three Chinese suspects denied all charges[289].

The Chinese side claimed that the project created 42,000 jobs and 92% employees were locals. By the end of 2016, the project had employed 8,976 Kenyan technical workers and 8,790 Kenyan management personnel, together accounting for 42.3% of the local employees[290]. However, Kenyan media exposed racism and discrimination against local workers; some locals were paid less than a quarter of what their Chinese counterparts earned for the same job; Kenyan workers were not allowed to share dining tables and commuting vehicles with Chinese workers; most gadgets were programmed in Chinese, thus the language barrier prevented Kenyan train drivers and technicians from mastering the machines; and Chinese instructors were reluctant to transfer skills to Kenyan trainees[291].

In January 2019, the details of the SRG contract were revealed by Kenyan media, leading to a new round of concerns about the project. Critics argued that Kenyan sovereignty is at great risk, for example since one clause implies that Kenya must forfeit its assets if it defaults on the loan, while another clause says any disputes on the loan will only be resolved in Beijing through the China International Economic and Trade Arbitration Commission[292].

CRBC signed a ten-year operation and maintenance contract with Kenya Railways in 2017, thus SRG will still be run by this company in the near future[293].

What kind of approach to development is China offering in Africa?

In the past, China has been seen as a friend and ally of many Africa countries against Western colonialism and Chinese aid has been welcomed. China has provided grants and loans (both concessional and non-concessional) and other resources to support development in Africa. Indeed, loans have been a major form of Chinese capital flow to Africa. Many have gone towards supporting major infrastructure construction projects that are often contracted to Chinese companies.

Debt

In 2000 China cancelled US$10 billion in debt owed by African countries and in 2003 it offered additional debt relief to 31 African countries[294]. Similarly, in September 2018, China announced that loans that had been given to 'Africa's least developed countries would be exempted and forgiven', although specific details were not provided[295]. Significant debts continue to exist, however, and the issue of the repayment terms of China's loans to African countries and how they will be repaid in the future still remains. Of 72 low income countries (including 40 African countries) for which the World Bank published data in 2020[296], 62% of debt owed to Chinese creditors was disbursed to African countries. For 32 of the 40 African countries, China was the biggest bilateral lender. Interestingly, besides from Angola (which had the largest debt owed to China of all 72 countries at US$19 million), the data shows a peak in Chinese lending in 2013 but that with the five to seven year grace period of a lot of Chinese loans, many countries may now be facing significant principle repayments[297].

While often presented as " assistance" or "aid" by China, the potential debt burden to African countries has been a cause for concern. The 'Angola model' is a term that became coined in 2008 to refer to a model of development along the lines of China's economic relations with Angola. In the mid-2000s, China identified Angola as a potential major supplier of oil, and this was at a time when, following the end of decades of civil war, Angola was in desperate need of rebuilding functioning infrastructure. China and Angola therefore made an agreement where Angola accepted oil-backed credit from China's Eximbank for the construction of infrastructure such as roads, hospitals, schools and housing. Not only did this benefit China through the provision of oil, around 70% of the infrastructure construction projects making use of the credit were assigned to Chinese companies[298]. This agreement later caused problems for Angola. It left the country without enough oil to sell on the open market for cash to put into the economy and triggered a massive inflation spike. Moreover, when the price of oil crashes, such as it did with the 2008 financial crisis, the contract with China means Angola is forced to borrow money to make up the difference that it owes, resulting in a debt problem[299].

While resource backed loans similar to those offered by China are not unique – Western banks made similar loans to African countries before this –China has been described as having "built the model to scale" and applying it systematically[300]. China used a similar model to secure cobalt and copper mining rights in the Democratic Republic of Congo in 2008 for instance. As this model has become increasingly criticized, some have suggested that China may now be trying to downplay the role of natural resources for Sino-African relations and move towards new models of economic cooperation. However recent loans to Ghana and Guinea where Chinese companies provide financing for infrastructure projects in exchange for bauxite have been questioned for posing debt risks, with one report pointing out that the repayment schedule would demand a rapid increase in bauxite production and refining[301].

Another problem with some Chinese loans in Africa is that even when they are 'concessional' or 'interest free' they might pose a greater risk of a debt burden than expected. According to Ching Kwan Lee in discussing Chinese investments in Zambia, Chinese concessional loans have higher rates of interest when compared to World Bank loans, smaller grant elements, shorter repayment periods and require noncompetitive single sourcing from China. She furthermore cites a senior technocrat from the Zambian Ministry of Finance as saying that, "their so-called interest-free loans actually carry other charges and fees that, taken together, amount to interest bearing loans"[302]. In 2018, fears were raised that Zambia's debt would lead to China taking over Zambia's national power supplier, Zesco, which has been used as a guarantee for loans. However, this is something that had not happened at the time of writing and Lubinda Haaabazoka, the President of the Economics Association of Zambia, has denied the risk[303], despite Zambia's external debt estimated to be at 35% of its GDP, and loans from China accounting for 65.8% of this debt according to the Brookings Institution estimates[304]. Several construction projects in Zambia involving Chinese companies have also recently been suspended due to financial difficulties.

Despite the potential debt risks, the way that China has also been seen as offering an alternative to a unipolar world associated with Western dominance, is another related reason cooperation with China has been welcomed by many political leaders in Africa. The example of China has also been viewed by some as a potential 'model' for how development can be achieved without 'Western democracy'. Although the idea that China offers a model to simply be applied to the development of other countries is something that has been increasingly rejected by Chinese officials.

Political implications, transparency and corruption

It is also worth observing how Chinese 'aid' or 'development assistance' has not only been in the form of grants, equipment and concessional loans, it has included the provision of scholarships and training[305]. As of 2007, China had cultural agreements with 42 African countries and 65 cultural exchange programmes and had offered scholarships to 10,000 students[306]. Beijing has also been inviting political and business figures to China for exchanges and training. Having already hosted 200 between 2011 and 2015, in 2016 Beijing announced that it would invite 1,000 young African politicians to China for training[307]. Some analysts have argued that the purpose of such exchanges is to help cultivate leaders that are more sympathetic to China.

Indeed, in addition to potentially leading to economic dependency on China, Chinese investments might be linked to political consequences. Following São Tomé and Príncipe cutting diplomatic ties with Taiwan and re-establishing ties with the PRC in 2016, China donated US$146 million for infrastructure construction to the island state[308]. Other countries, such as Chad and Malawi, have had to cut ties with Taiwan (a prerequisite for establishing ties with China) to pursue trade and investment relations with China.

China also built the US$200 million headquarters of the African Union in Addis Ababa, which opened in 2012. Later, claims that it was being used for spying emerged when it was reported that data from computers in the headquarters were being transferred to China each night. China denied that it had hacked the headquarters[309].

One problem in assessing conditions attached to Chinese loans and investment is that there is often a lack of transparency, secrecy or in some cases indications of corrupt practices in the negotiations and conclusion of trade and investment deals involving China and African countries. In December 2018, a US federal jury found former Hong Kong Home Secretary Patrick Ho Chi-Ping guilty of bribery and money laundering over oil rights in Chad and Uganda for former energy conglomerate CEFC China Energy. Ho was found to have offered US$2.9 million in bribes to Chad President Idriss Déby, Sengalese diplomat Cheikh Gadio and Ugandan foreign minister Sam Kutesa[310]. Mysteries also surround some operations by Chinese companies including, for instance, of Sam Pa (a businessman with seven names who is believed to have connections to Chinese intelligence and SOEs) and the Queensway Group (a group of companies all connected to an address at 88 Queensway in Hong Kong) and their investment in Africa[311]. Corruption and lack of transparency not only make it ever more difficult to hold companies accountable, it fuels suspicions about China's intentions, and also further calls into question whose interests such cross-border investments really serve. This is especially so given that bribery has also reportedly been used in some cases to buy off local government or union officials, while those who speak out against poor working conditions have been threatened. In 2010 Chinese managers reportedly fired shotguns at a crowd of protesting workers from a copper mine in Sinazongwe Zambia[312].

Impacts on people and the environment

In addition to debt problems, political implications and a lack of transparency, some sections of civil society have been concerned about Africa's relationship with China and the impact that it has on human rights and humanitarian conditions. Its arms sales, for instance, are often cheaper than those from Western countries and do not usually have the same human rights and humanitarian conditions imposed. During the Sudan crisis, for instance, this meant support for a military regime involved in ethnic cleansing , while it has also provided the Mugabe regime in Zimbabwe with financial aid, machinery and military supplies .

A lack of protection of the rights and interests of workers employed by Chinese companies operating in Africa, including on infrastructure construction projects is another problem that has been criticized. According to a Building and Woodworkers International resolution on workers' rights in Chinese multinational companies passed in May 2013:

The Chinese MNCs in several African nations, and in Nepal and Pakistan, have exhibited a general disrespect to workers' rights and labour standards - discrimination in wages of local and Chinese workers, poor housing facilities, non-compliance with local labour laws, lack of / inadequate social security cover and poor OHS conditions that characterise Chinese MNCs worksites[313].

While many Chinese projects in Africa hire management and supervisors from China but a large proportion of the workforce locally, for concessional loans projects a larger number of Chinese workers may be permitted as part of the agreement[314]. This is something that has sometimes been reported to cause resentment among local workers, including when pay and conditions are believed to be different, something which may be exacerbated by limited interactions and language barriers between workers. Nevertheless, a recent study that compared Chinese and non-Chinese manufacturing and construction companies in Ethiopia and Angola found that Chinese companies mostly employ similar numbers of local workers as non-Chinese companies operating in these countries and pay and train them more or less the same. In Ethiopia, almost 90% of employees at Chinese companies were local, and for unskilled labour Chinese companies were hiring entirely locally. In Angola, which had higher levels of skill shortages, both Chinese and non-Chinese companies employed a lower percentage of local labour, although for Chinese companies the percentage of local employees had risen to 74% from 50% about a decade earlier[315].

As in Asia, some of the investments and activities of Chinese companies in Africa have also been potentially destructive to the environment and led to the destruction of farmland and homes. In the mid-2000s, Sinopec's prospecting for oil led to mass pollution and destruction of the country's national parks and rainforests, causing public outrage. In some cases, Chinese companies have been fined by overseas governments as a result of the damage caused to the environment. In 2014, for instance the Chad government fined China National Petroleum Corporation (CNPC) US$1.2 billion and revoked its oil license for environmental damages due to the dumping of excess crude oil. The fine was subsequently commuted to US$400 million, however this coincides with allegations that former Hong Kong Home Secretary Patrick Ho, who was later convicted of seven counts of bribery and money laundering over oil rights in Africa by US courts, had asked Senegalese diplomat Cheikh Gadio to help resolve the issue.

Where homes and livelihoods have been destroyed residents have not always been adequately compensated. Demolition of homes to make way for the Lagos-Ibadan railway in Nigeria, funded by Exim and to be built by China Civil Engineering Construction Company, for example, came under criticism for the lack of compensation to residents. Harm to lands and homes of local residents has sometimes led to protests that have s brought a halt to operations by Chinese companies. In October 2016, Chinese company Jiuxing mines had to halt its activities (for which it had received a 40-year license) in Soamahamanina in Madagascar due to protests by locals whose lands were being affected[316].

Risky prospects

Given the numerous problems associated with Chinese investments in Africa for the host countries concerned, it is perhaps unsurprising that there are many examples of mega-projects that have resulted in failure, cancellation or delay as opposition, disagreement or practical difficulties in implementation emerge. Examples include, cancelled railway projects in Nigeria and Libya, petroleum expansion in Angola and Nigeria, melting and smelting investments in the Democratic Republic of the Congo and Ghana and a US$100 billion hydropower project on the Congo river being put on hold[317]. Some projects have also resulted in losses, the Addis Ababa-Djibouti railway, for instance, cost Sinosure almost US$1 billion in losses. Meanwhile, although at the 2015 FOCAC, The China Africa Industrial Capacity Cooperation Fund was announced with the intention of giving US$10 billion to invest in big low-risk projects, by 2018 only six projects worth $542 million had been approved and local African companies had not been the beneficiaries of any of them[318]. While China and Chinese companies have multiple reasons for pursuing the expansion of investment overseas, and the type of development promoted by China is one in which China itself likely stands to gain more than host countries, its investments in Africa are very far from risk free. Indeed, in October 2018, the South China Morning Post reported China Export and Credit Insurance Corporation (Sinosure[319]) head, Wang Wen, as saying that Chinese developers and financiers involved with BRI projects in developing countries needed to increase their risk management if they wanted to avoid disaster[320].

Part 7: China's investments in Asia[321]

Global concern about the implications of China's increasing investments overseas has been felt not least in Asia. Given its close regional proximity to China, Asia is a region where China has significantly upgraded efforts to try to assert a leading role, not only for economic benefit but also to gain strategic leverage and attempt to counter US hegemony. While increased Chinese overseas investment in Africa has early received much more attention, the growth of China's economic activities in Asia have also become increasingly notable not only for their potential political implications but also for the way that they have been reshaping the lives of ordinary people and threatened the environment.

Types of investment in Asia

One significant form of investment that has grown in terms of value in Asia is China's FDI. According to official statistics, by the end of 2018 the value of China's FDI stock in Asia amounted to almost US$1.3 trillion compared with just over US$447 trillion at the end of 2013. While globally, developed economies still dominate among major recipient countries of Chinese FDI, this is beginning to change. There has been a growth in Chinese FDI to all continents since 2001, and Asia has received a substantial proportion of it[322]. One major reason for this is the inclusion of Hong Kong, which continues to receive by far the largest proportion of mainland China's outbound FDI. Growth in FDI to Asia is also in line with a general trend in the growth of Asia's global importance as a destination for inward FDI (not only from China). Asia's share of the global total of FDI stocks rose by 9.6 percentage points between 2005 and 2015 to reach 23.8%[323]. Nevertheless, although in terms of value Chinese FDI in Asia has been continuing to grow, in recent years outbound FDI to Asia has declined as a percentage of China's total global FDI.

As a large and diverse continent, the significance of Chinese FDI flows to Asia has varied by region and country, however, and major statistical discrepancies make a clear picture difficult to obtain, although there seems to be consensus on a general trend of growth in value. In Southeast Asia, for instance, despite geographic proximity, China's FDI has been comparatively small as a percentage of China's total global FDI. In 2013, China only contributed a total of 2.3% of its FDI into ASEAN[324]. However, Singapore, as a more developed country, receives a significant proportion of Chinese FDI to the region and ranks amongst the leading individual recipient globally of Chinese FDI (see table below), with its FDI to the country more than tripling from US$4,857 million to US$14,751 million between 2009 to 2013. It is thought, however, that some of this FDI to Singapore then flows to other ASEAN countries[325]. Other leading Asian recipient countries or regions of Chinese FDI have included Cambodia, Kazakhstan, Indonesia, Macau, Myanmar, Mongolia, South Korea and Pakistan. Even where, by global comparison, the amounts received may be small, for some countries Chinese FDI may still account for a significant proportion of all FDI received by the country concerned.

As a part of its investment activity, the growth of China's outbound FDI has received a lot of attention globally. While this is a trend that is replicated in terms of value in Asia, Chinese overseas lending to the region is also very significant. Moreover, closely related to such Chinese investment, a large proportion of China's economic activity results from commercial contracts (for instance in infrastructure construction). The award of such contracts to Chinese companies are sometimes a condition of Chinese lending. These loans and contracts are an important feature of the infrastructure investments being driven in association with the BRI.

Between 2000 and 2014, five Asian countries (Pakistan received $16.3 billion, Laos $11 billion, Turkmenistan $10.1 billion, Sri Lanka $8.2 billion and Kazakhstan $6.7 billion) were amongst the top ten countries to receive financing from China classified as 'other official flows' (OOF), meaning that they were non- concessional or commercial in nature. Top sectors for overall OOF from China during this period were energy generation and supply (51%), transport and storage (17%), industry, mining and construction (10%), communications (5%) and agriculture, forestry and fishing (3%)[326]. In other words, even before the BRI was fully underway, infrastructure was an important component of China's official financing overseas and was significant in Asia. With the increased political push from the BRI and commitments to this by the Chinese banks, such lending and the associated debt that will need to be repaid might likely be expected to increase. Indeed, according to one estimate, between 2013 and early 2020 the total announced lending[327] by Chinese financial institutions to BRI projects totaled US$461 billion, with Indonesia, Pakistan and Iran among top recipients[328]. With the coronavirus pandemic causing economic hardship in many countries around the world from 2020, there has been increasing concern about debt burdens and calls from some BRI countries for debt relief by some countries, for instance Pakistan. While Beijing was reportedly considering a number of responses, including suspension of interest payments, a researcher from China Development Bank reportedly told the Financial Times that:

The BRI loans are not foreign aid. We need to at least recoup principal and a moderate interest… It is OK for 20 per cent of our portfolio projects to have problems. But we can't tolerate half of them going under. We might consider extending loans and giving interest relief. But in general, our loans are issued according to market principles[329].

As far as conventional aid is concerned, this is less significant. During the 2000 to 2014 period, the countries which received the greatest amount of conventional Chinese aid were mainly in Africa, however Cambodia and Sri Lanka were also ranked in the top ten global recipients receiving US$3 billion and US$2.8 billion in ODA respectively[330].

As previously mentioned, Chinese lending to finance large infrastructure projects is often accompanied by the award of contracts to Chinese companies for the construction of the respective infrastructure. This is especially so in Asia. Based on official statistical data, Asian countries account for a significant proportion of the value of projects contracted by Chinese companies overseas. In 2016, for instance, the value of Chinese contracts in Asia accounted for 48% of the total value of Chinese contracted projects globally. Saudi Arabia, from where China receives a significant proportion of its oil imports and with which it has recently signed agreements and letters of intent worth $65bn in energy, space and infrastructure agreements, has granted Chinese companies the greatest value of contracts, accounting for 12% of the value of contracts from all Asian countries in 2016. Meanwhile Pakistan, where China is making significant investment in the China-Pakistan Economic Corridor, accounts for the second highest value amounting to 9% of the total for Asia. In recent years, construction, transportation and real estate are areas that have seen significant growth in the value of contracts in Asia in particular. The value of transportation projects contracted in Asia grew from $16.2 billion from 2006 to 2011 to $62.03 billion from 2012 to 2017, whereas the value of contracted real estate projects grew from $9.2 billion from 2006 to 2011 to $21.1 billion from 2012 to 2017[331].

Incentives

In addition to the general incentives and reasons for promoting overseas investment set out in Part One of this report, there are also some incentives for expanding investment and related activities that are specific to Asia. On the one hand, lower wages (including lower minimum wages) and other benefits in some countries when compared with China have been additional factors that make investing in developing countries in Asia more attractive to Chinese companies (a similar factor drove the massive influx of foreign capital into China from the 1990s). Chinese overseas investment in the Cambodian garment sector offers one such example[332]. Perhaps more significantly, however, regional geopolitical interests and a desire to establish itself as a dominant power in the region in the face of rival competitors such as the US and Japan, may also be considered a motivating factor for establishing closer economic relations and encouraging some countries to increasingly rely on China.

Indeed, Xi Jinping has talked about wanting to create 'an Asia-Pacific dream for our people'. In 2013 China's foreign minister, Wang Yi, announced that the focus of China's foreign policy would move to China's backyard, where it wants to build, "a community of shared destiny"[333]. These comments, which seemingly present a unified goal (implicitly China-led) perhaps run somewhat in contrast with China's generally stated approach to foreign policy, whereby it insists on opposition to unilateralism, non-interference into the affairs of each country and its respect for differences. More broadly, the term tianchao zhuyi, which loosely translates as heavily dynastism, has been used by liberal critics to refer to China's ambitions and activities overseas. Debates have also arisen around suggestions that China is now imperialist or is in the process of returning to the role of an imperialist power. While this is a debate that requires further consideration elsewhere, in its own backyard, where it vies for political and economic influence in the face of regional and international rivals, attempts to establish itself as a regional hegemonic power are increasingly evident, not only through its economic activities but also as witnessed through its increasingly aggressive strategies in the South China Sea. The waters represent significant channels of communication and trade. Almost 40% of all China's trade passes through the south china sea, as well as significant proportions for other countries[334]. While several countries (including China) make territorial claims to the contested waters and islands in the South China Sea, since 2013 China has been constructing artificial islands around the Spratley and Paracel islands and has expanded its military presence, a sign of it more strongly asserting its claim to sovereignty which has exacerbated tensions in the region. Matters have not been helped by the interventions of countries such as the US and UK, which have provoked China further by carrying out warship sailing operations through the disputed waters (seen as a potential threat and undermining China's claims). More recently, declining US-China relations have led to increasing tensions over the South China Sea, which have led some to speculate or fear potential future military clashes in the region.

There is, however, a way to go before China becomes the sole major force in the region. With an economy measuring US$10.9 trillion in 2015 (larger than other East and Southeast Asian economies combined), and as a major trading partner of many Asian countries, China already has very significant economic leverage. Nevertheless, although the BRI has been viewed as a way to further boost regional investment, it is not necessarily the dominant actor throughout the region. The EU and Japan, for instance, were investing more overall in Southeast Asia than China when the BRI was announced[335]. Between 2011-2013, the EU invested US75 billion and Japan invested US56 billion, while China invested the lower amount of US$22 billion in ASEAN countries. Meanwhile, Japan remains the largest provider of aid (where it is defined as grants and loans at minimal interest rates) to Southeast Asia. Successfully driving forward the BRI therefore may be viewed as a way to enable it to be more assertive in view of the comparative strength of its competitors. Indeed, this is something which has not gone unnoticed. China's growing investments and influence in the region may have prompted responses in the form of increased investments from states and associated institutions that see China as a rival for economic and political influence in the region. Following plans for the BRI and AIIB being outlined, in 2015 Japan's Prime Minister Shinzo Abe announced that Japan would provide US$110 billion for Asian infrastructure over the next five years, while the ADB expanded its lending capacity by 50%. Then in July 2018, US Secretary of State, Mike Pompeo, announced a new infrastructure initiative in the Asia-Pacific region, the 'Indo-Pacific Economic-Vision', to involve US$113 million in direct government investment in infrastructure, energy and new technology[336]. The US, Australia and Japan also announced that they had formed a trilateral partnership to mobilise investments in energy, transportation, tourism and technology infrastructure[337].

Problems with China's investments in Asia

Infrastructure in parts of Asia is underdeveloped and in this respect infrastructure investments might be welcomed. Indeed, China has often presented its investments as a 'win-win situation', previously projecting, for instance, that Southeast Asian countries had plans to invest US$1.5 trillion in infrastructure between 2011 and 2020 and could therefore benefit from Chinese investment[338]. As far as overseas governments are concerned, in many instances, China's overseas ambitions to invest in infrastructure are viewed as a way to gain the capital to meet the infrastructure and development aims of the respective country's government. The Thai government, for instance, has sought Chinese investment and integration with the BRI for its own Eastern Economic Corridor development plan. Under this plan Thailand hopes to attract US$46 billion in foreign investment (not only from China), for development of train, rail, road and marine transportation and investment in strategic industries such as biotechnology, biofuel, IT, medicine and aviation, for which it has reportedly offered investors additional corporate and personal income tax privileges[339]. Related to this, construction of the first phase of the China-Thailand high speed railway, seen by China as a flagship project of the BRI, began in late 2017, albeit after some delay due to disagreement over the loan that China Development Bank was offering the Thai government to finance the project[340]. China is also expected to be a key financier in Duterte's 'Build, Build, Build' infrastructure project in the Philippines. Meanwhile, in Cambodia, where China is the country's largest foreign investor, the government has continued to seek aid and investment for infrastructure such as bridge and road construction, in the face of rising concern from civil society about some of the adverse impacts[341] that have also been the cause of growing anti-Chinese sentiment[342]. In Pakistan, however, one of the criticisms levied against the CPEC relates to lack of transparency in investment allocation and the Pakistan central government giving preferential treatment to some provinces along the eastern route and denying other areas the benefits of the investments[343].

The CPEC in particular has received a lot of criticism from those that claim that the loans are not economically viable, and Pakistan will likely have a hard time meeting its repayment obligations. The IMF, for instance, previously warned that when Chinese investors start repatriating profits and after 2021 when repayments are expected to rise, if the CPEC does not generate enough growth, then Pakistan's debt from Chinese bank loans risk becoming a burden[344]. More recently, Pakistan's overall debt levels have contributed to economic crisis prompting the Pakistan government to approach the IMF for a bailout.

In addition to Pakistan, a study by the Center for Global Development has identified seven other BRI countries (the majority in Asia) that face significant risk of debt distress due to high levels of debt owed to China, with some potentially at risk of having to default especially if further loans are made. These countries include Kyrgyzstan, Mongolia and Laos, Maldives, Djibouti, Montenegro, Tajikistan and Mongolia[345]. Such risks have already turned out to be a real problem for some countries. In Sri Lanka, for instance, the inability to repay debts to China has already resulted in the country having to cede majority control over the Hambantota port in exchange for debt relief, leading to major protests in 2017[346].

While debt may cause challenges for overseas countries, the impacts may not always[347] be so detrimental to China. Chinese loans have also provided a way to secure land, resources and further contracts for Chinese companies. Some loans by Chinese banks to overseas countries are backed by natural resources, a notable example being oil, meaning that the country may be required to pay off the debt using the resource, regardless of the domestic need. The same is true of infrastructure as in the case of Sri Lanka. There are also examples of cases, for instance in Cambodia, where repayment of debt is allegedly rescheduled or cancelled in exchange for Chinese companies being awarded further contracts[348].

In Asia, there have been situations that suggest that some countries might be more likely to take favourable political lines towards China in exchange for investment. Cambodia received US$600 million in development aid and loans in 2016 shortly after calling for ASEAN to retract its statement of the South China Sea dispute. It has also reportedly made exemptions to its laws for China, awarding land to Chinese companies far exceeding legal limits, coinciding with loans and investments[349]. In Myanmar, China has also allegedly directly tried to involve itself in the conflict issues faced by the country. In 2013 China designated a special envoy of diplomats, which continues to facilitate talks between armed organizations and the Myanmar government. China has also defended the Myanmar government over Rakhine state, an area where China has significant economic interests related to infrastructure and a planned Special Economic Zone, and where armed forces have carried out ethnic cleansing of the Rohingya population[350]. Chinese diplomats have denied involvement in the conflict, although admitted that there have been, "individual acts that broke the law of either country or affected the peace process of Myanmar" that were unrelated to China's policies[351]. Regardless of more direct political intervention, however, concerns have also been raised more recently about the debt implications for Myanmar related to plans to build the Kyaukpyu port, without it facing similar risks to those that have already affected Sri Lanka. When countries become trapped in debt and have to give up their resources, or if they adapt laws and environmental regulations to attract Chinese investment then this already has potential political implications for the countries concerned.

As in cases involving capital from other overseas countries, labour rights violations are frequently reported at Chinese companies and in Chinese invested operations in Asian countries. One issue which has become especially contentious for some countries in Asia, however, is the use of Chinese workers for projects contracted to Chinese companies. Indeed, Asian countries receive a high percentage of all Chinese workers sent overseas in relation to contracts awarded to Chinese companies. According to data from official statistics, in 2016 61% of Chinese dispatch workers sent overseas to work on contracted projects were sent to Asian countries, while a total of 46% of Chinese persons abroad related to contracted projects were in Asian countries at the end of the year. It should also be noted, however, that official statistics only provide data on the number of workers sent overseas through legal channels, such as overseas labour cooperation companies and employment agencies licensed by the Ministry of Commerce. Workers are also sometimes sent by unlicensed agencies and labour brokers[352], and so the actual number is likely much higher. Tensions have emerged where the local population have felt that Chinese workers were being employed at the expense of the employment of local workers, and this, along with other complaints related to Chinese investments, has contributed to growing anti-Chinese sentiments or racism in several Southeast Asian countries including Laos, Indonesia, the Philippines and Vietnam.

Nevertheless, infringements of labour rights not only affect local workers but also the Chinese workers imported to work on contracted projects (especially when they are imported through illegal channels). Indeed, many overseas Chinese workers have faced exploitation and rights violations at the hands of the Chinese contracted or investing company as well as the labour dispatch employment agency. Unpaid wages and visa issues have been amongst problems that they have faced. In 2017, for instance, Malaysian media reported that Chinese migrant workers working on the construction of the Forest City project in Malaysia were facing wage arrears and had not been provided with the proper work visas after being cheated by agents in China to whom they needed to repay huge loans[353].

Land use is another major issue in Asia. Myanmar is one country where problems related to land use as a result of Chinese invested projects have surfaced. From 1988 to 2010, during the military period, many land intensive infrastructure projects were approved in Myanmar without safeguards for communities and the environment, of which a large number involved investments by Chinese SOEs[354]. However, Myanmar is also an example of a country where Chinese investments have frequently met significant public opposition related to these issues. In 2011, the construction of a US$3.7 billion Chinese backed hydro dam project was halted due to opposition, then later in the year a Chinese backed copper-mine project was also temporarily put on hold following protests. The Sino-Myanmar pipeline project has also been met with opposition from local communities due to negative impacts on livelihoods and inadequate compensation for loss of land. The Chinese invested Letpadaung Copper Mine has also been a site of several protests that have often been met with violent repression[355] due to land seizures, dissatisfaction over the compensation offered to villagers for resettlement and pollution. It has subsequently been argued that in view of earlier experiences, including the backlash from civil society as well as changing political circumstances and insecurity in the region, the Chinese government and some Chinese companies are attempting to improve relationships with communities and minimize conflict by engaging with different stakeholders[356], although the effectiveness remains to be seen.

It is not just humans that have been affected by inadequate assessments and consideration of environmental impacts; ecological destruction also endangers wildlife. In the Batang Toru rainforest on Sumatra in Indonesia, the development of a US$1.6 billion hydroelectric dam has raised concerns due to the threat it poses to the habitat of the endangered Tapanuli orangutan and the Sumatran tiger. The power plant, which is being developed by Indonesia company PT North Sumatra Hydro Energy, is reportedly backed by the Bank of China, while Sinohydro (the SOE that built the Three Gorges Dam) has been awarded the contract for design and construction. According to conservationists, the threat to the orangutans was given little attention in the project's environmental impact assessment and the Indonesian Forum for the Environment (Walhi) filed a legal challenge against the project's environmental permit in August 2018. The environmentalists also reportedly claim that while the Bank of China continues to back the project, the World Bank dropped out due to environmental concerns[357]. The dam project has also led to protests by indigenous people, for instance in August 2017, when faced with eviction from their land, dozens protested against the project leading to violent clashes with representatives of the developer and police[358].

Gwadar Port (Pakistan) – a strategic and challenging case

One project that has been included in the BRI and is especially strategic to China but is also problematic and challenging as far as ordinary people and the environment are concerned is the case of Gwadar Port.

Gwadar is located on the southwestern coast of Pakistan's Balochistan province, about 460 kilometers east of Karachi and about 120 km west of the Pakistan-Iran border. It is near the Strait of Hormuz and close to several important strategic maritime routes linking the Persian Gulf and Asia Pacific[359]. Building a deep sea port in Gwadar had been Pakistan's dream for quite a long time, but the plan was only implemented after China agreed to offer help at the end of the 1990s[360]. In March 2002, China Harbour Engineering Company (CHEC) and the Ministry of Ports and Shipping of Pakistan signed a contract to construct Phase 1 of Gwadar Port, costing US$248 million[361]. China provided US$198 million. It is difficult to find out the details of this investment, however, and public reports only say that it included grants, interest-free loans, concessional loans and buyer credits[362].

Chinese workers were involved in the port's construction and some became victims of terrorist attacks. In May 2004, a commuting van was targeted by a car bomb on its way to the construction site of Phase 1. Three Chinese engineers were killed on the spot and nine Chinese workers were injured. Two Pakistani workers in the same van, a driver and a security guard were also injured[363]. Later Pakistan's police arrested 13 suspects in connection with this attack[364].

Phase 1 was completed in 2006 and the Port of Singapore Authority (PSA) won the bid to become the port's operator in the same year[365]. The original lease was for 40 years; however, PSA ended the US$750 million deal in 2012 for two major reasons:

Firstly, the security situation in Balochistan hindered the PSA from investing the money it had promised in the agreement for the development of the port and offshore infrastructure.

Secondly, the Supreme Court [of Pakistan] had issued a stay order against the allotment of Gwadar land to a foreign company, back in December 2010, on petitions filed by some individuals, including the Balochistan governor[366].

In February 2013, however, a contract for construction and operation of Gwadar Port was awarded to China Overseas Port Holding Company (COPHC). President Asif Ali Zardari and Chinese Ambassador Liu Jian attended the contract signing ceremony, indicating that this was highly important to both countries. However, COPHC, the company awarded the contract, is a mysterious company that little is known about—the address of its parent company in Hong Kong is one single room shared by four different companies, a typical sign of a shell or paper company. There is also no public information showing the existence of any contenders in this deal[367]. The lack of transparency around this deal might be considered worrying.

The importance of this project for China nevertheless became further apparent shortly afterwards. Later in the same year, China and Pakistan reached a consensus on building the long-planned China-Pakistan Economic Corridor (CPEC)[368] and plans for the BRI were also announced by Xi Jinping. The development of Gwadar Port has been integrated into these initiatives since then and is considered a flagship project of CPEC.

In November 2016, Gwadar Port officially opened, but further constructions and upgrades are still on-going. China Communications Construction Company (CCCC) has also since been awarded contracts related to Gwadar Port. In March 2017, for example, the Pakistani government awarded the 300-megawatt coal power project at Gwadar, which was worth 55 billion PKR, to CCCC without bidding[369]; and in September 2017, it signed the Gwadar East Bay Expressway project contract[370].

It has been suggested that Gwadar Port is advantageous to China since it will allow China to benefit from a shorter transportation route for the transportation of oil and gas from gulf countries. In the case that potential conflicts in the Asia-Pacific region, especially in the South China Sea, arise, alternative energy supply routes could be beneficial[371].

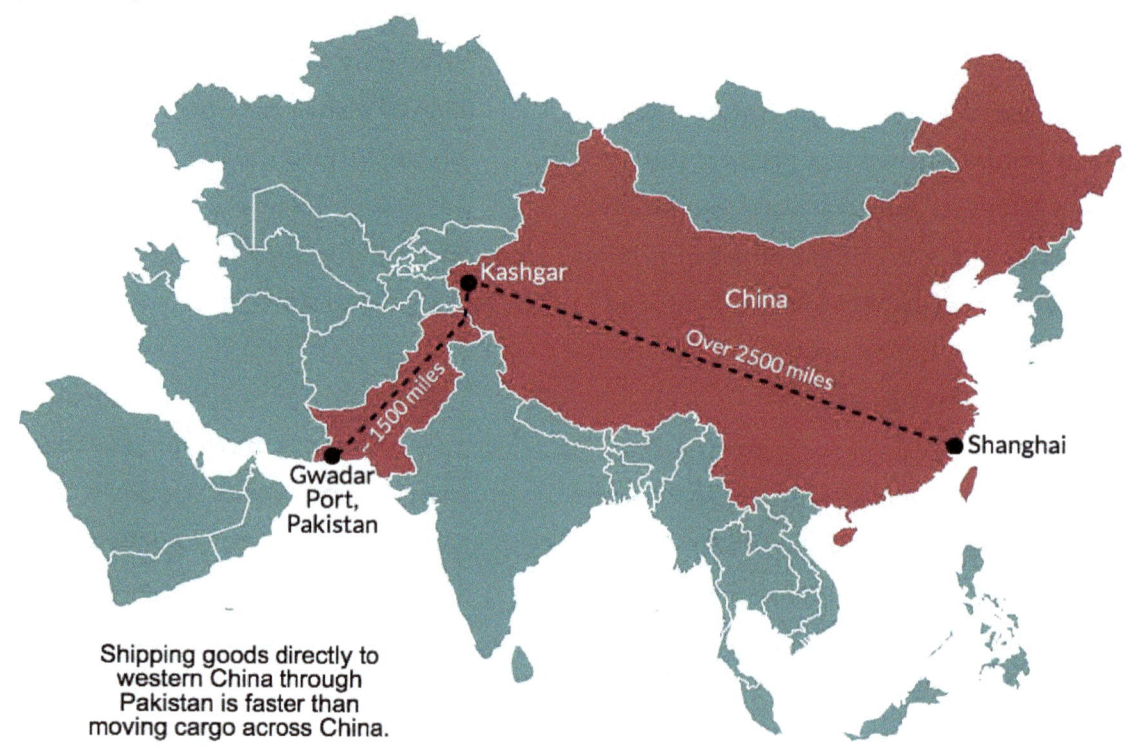

Strategic cargo route from Gwadar Port to western China

Shipping goods directly to western China through Pakistan is faster than moving cargo across China.

Source: China Dialogue Ocean[372]

Nevertheless, the development of Gwadar Port and CPEC are not appreciated by everyone in Gwadar. One issue is the displacement of local fishing communities. COPHC promised that it would create as many as two million jobs in 20 years. However, local fishermen worry that they don't have the necessary skills to compete with workers from the other parts of Pakistan and even from China. They also complain that the government has not fulfilled its promises related to compensation, schools, hospital and roads after it gave up land to the project[373].

Chinese projects are also facing security problems caused by general instability in Balochistan province, threatening Chinese workers and locals. The 2004 incident mentioned above was not the only attack targeting Chinese investment and companies. In November 2005, unidentified armed men fired five rockets at the camp site of a Chinese construction company in Gwadar. Two rockets landed and exploded in the parking area of the camp and damaged a number of vehicles. However, no casualties were reported in the attack[374]. In October

2017, unidentified men threw a grenade into a workers' hostel in Gwadar Port and wounded 26 workers who were having dinner[375]. Many of these attacks were carried out by Baloch separatists, who have been fighting against the central government in Islamabad for the liberation of the western Balochistan province for decades. Now they are also condemning China for plundering Balochistan's resources[376]. Another issue that has concerned both separatists and many ordinary Baloch people is that these CPEC-related projects will bring about a demographic change in the near future and turn them into a minority group in their own province[377].

Meanwhile, heavy-handed repression of China's Muslims in Xinjiang is also stirring up anti-China sentiments in Pakistan, which has driven religious extremists to act against Chinese citizens in Pakistan[378].

The dangers of debt to China? – the Hambantota Port case (Sri Lanka)

The case of Hambantota Port has been widely cited as a reason to be cautious about Chinese overseas investments. The plan to construct a port at Hambantota was proposed as early as 2002. However, the government only started implementing it after Mahina Rajapaksa became president in 2005. Rajapaksa was born in Hambantota and the region was his electoral district. Thus, he made election promises to create prosperity there[379].

Only China was willing to finance the project, however, as many other potential investors thought that building a new port did not make sense economically——the capacity of Sri Lanka's existing ports, such as Colombo, Galle, and Trincomalee, were still adequate[380]. Critics argued that China's consideration was geopolitical rather than economical—the new port could become its strategic foothold and navy base in the Indian Ocean[381].

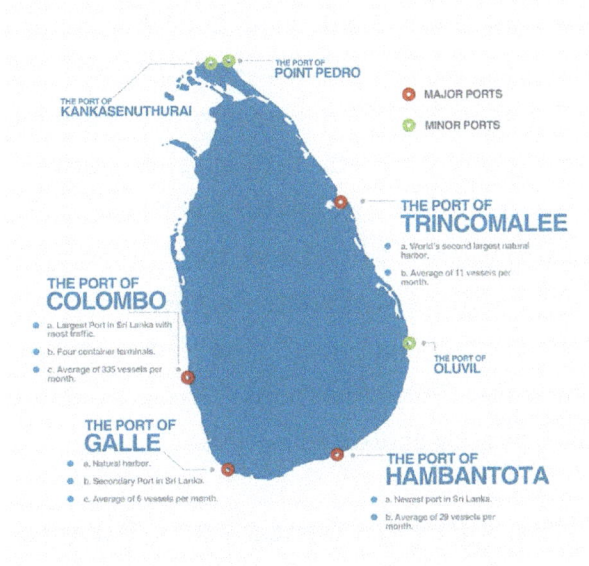

Ports of Sir Lanka. [382]Source: MMS

It is difficult to find all of the details of the negotiations between the two sides. Two Chinese SOEs, China Harbour Engineering Company (CHEC), a CCCC subsidiary, and Sinohydro, constructed Phase 1 of the project costing 361 million USD[383]. 85% of the cost, or 306 million USD, was paid with a 15-year loan from the Export-Import Bank of China, at a 6.3% interest rate[384]; and construction commenced in January 2008 and was completed by November 2010[385]. In December 2010, CHEC and the Sri Lanka Ports Authority then signed the EPC contract for Phase 2[386], which was to be entirely financed by the Export-Import Bank of China[387]. Construction of Phase 2 was completed by the end of 2016[388]. The total cost of the port's construction was 1.761 billion USD[389].

The Hambantota port was an economic disaster. During the first couple of years of operation it was unable to attract passing vessels and its profits were not enough to pay off the loans. By the end of 2016, the port's total losses had reached 304 million USD[390].

Rajapaksa lost the election in 2015, but the new government found that it was hard to repay the foreign debts—by 2015, some 95 percent of Sri Lanka's government revenue was going towards servicing its debts[391]. After months of negotiations with China, Sri Lanka agreed to hand over the Hambantota port to China Merchants Port Holdings Co., Ltd on a 99-year lease[392]. The latter's parent company, China Merchants Group, is also a SOE directly controlled by SASAC.

Changing fortunes for Chinese investments in Asia?

As this chapter has highlighted, there has been a growth in Chinese investments and related economic activity in Asia, accompanying the increased strategic importance of the expansion of China's overseas expansion and the BRI by the Chinese state. While welcomed by some overseas governments, where Chinese investments have aligned with their own plans and interests, Chinese investment has nevertheless not met with universal enthusiasm. Concerns about some of the adverse effects of Chinese investment, the mounting costs to the countries involved, increasing anti-Chinese sentiment and popular backlash related to the growth and impacts of Chinese investment, along with the election of politicians that have adopted positions less favourable to such investment; have resulted in delay and even cancellation of projects. Disputes have also frequently occurred between Chinese investors and the countries in which they invest, some of which are brought to arbitration in Hong Kong. Last year the Hong Kong International Arbitration Centre recorded a 17% rise in the number of disputes that it handled involving mainland Chinese parties and parties from other BRI countries[393].

A prominent recent example of the reversal in fortune for Chinese investment overseas following a change in government comes from Malaysia and its halting of the construction of the East Coast Rail Link after costs greatly exceeded original estimates. With most of the work on the planned 620-kilometre railway line awarded to China Communication Construction Company (CCCC) and 85% of the financing being provided by China's Exim bank, the project was supposed to connect the East Coast of Malaysia with Kuala Lumpur and Thailand, and aid in creating a trade route connecting China with markets beyond Asia. By late 2017, the project had been hailed the largest ongoing project by a Chinese company overseas, however in July 2018, Malaysia suspended the project with concerns having been cited about the project's costs and the borrowing from China that would have been required to complete it[394]. The suspension of the project came following the election of new Malaysian Prime Minister Mahathir Mohamad, who had promised to curb China's influence and to renegotiate some of the terms of the estimated US$34 billion worth of deals Malaysia had signed with China under predecessor Najib Razak[395], a big supporter of the BRI. This type of U-turn is not unique to Malaysia, however. The Nepalese government has also cancelled plans for Chinese companies to build hydroelectric plants in the country. In November 2017, it scrapped a US$2.5 billion deal for a Chinese company to build a plant on the Budhi Gandaki river, and then in May 2018 it announced that it would build a plant on West Seti river, which was previously to be constructed by China's Three Gorges International Corporation, by itself. The recent change in leadership in Pakistan has also been considered a potential cause for concern for the future of CPEC.

Now, with the Covid-19 pandemic causing significant economic hardship for people and countries around the world, those countries that are deeply in debt, be it to China or elsewhere, may face even greater risks of debt distress going forward. The long-term implications for China's BRI projects in Asia remain to be seen.

Part 8: Chinese Investment in Germany[396]

Germany has been one of the major recipients of Chinese overseas investment amongst European countries and, despite the increasing diversification of its investments more recently to other European countries, it is still considered one of the most appealing destinations for Chinese FDI. Between 2000 and 2015, Germany received a cumulative total of EUR 7,905 million in Chinese FDI, ranking fourth in the EU for this period in terms of investment received[397]. In the mid-2000s, investment was mostly in small greenfield projects, however since 2011 in particular investments have soared[398]. From 2011 to 2016 the value of Chinese investments in German companies grew from 690 million Euros to 7 billion Euros, although 4.5 billion of this total resulted from Midea's acquisition of Kuka[399]. In 2018, even while an overall decline in investment into Europe was reported, Chinese investment in Germany grew in terms of its total value[400]. As China has sought to expand international connectivity and transportation routes to Europe as part of the BRI, Germany has also been integrated as a destination for trains departing from China to Europe included in this initiative.

Since Germany is a country which has been so important to China as it has expanded its investments into Europe, Globalization Monitor was keen to learn more about how Chinese investment is viewed there and the impacts it has had so far, particularly in the workplace. For this reason, in November 2018 we visited Germany for two weeks to meet with works council members, trade unionists and other activists and experts about their experiences related to Chinese investment and visited strategic sites of interest for Chinese investment activity. Our visit took us to two different locations in Germany. The first was North Rheine-Westphalia[401], an early industrial area, where Chinese companies have been acquiring manufacturing plants in various industries and where the city of Duisburg has received recent attention in relation to its role for China's new Silk Road as the terminal of its rail route from Chongqing. The second location was Hamburg, a city which has been an important location for the establishment of the European headquarters of Chinese companies – 500 such headquarters are now located there[402]—and where plans to construct a new container terminal at its port, to potentially be built and operated by Chinese companies, have become a cause for concern. This report draws on our discussions and findings from this visit as well relevant recent reports and literature to explore some of the important emerging issues for understanding implications of Chinese investment in Germany, as well as potentially further afield.

How has China been investing in Germany?

Map of Germany

Source: http://ontheworldmap.com/germany/germany-political-map.html

Chinese companies have made numerous investments in Germany of various sizes. In 2016, for instance, 68 acquisitions were made by Chinese companies in Germany[403]. One of the main reasons is its advanced manufacturing capabilities. Germany has been seen as a location from which China might not only benefit from the acquisition of industrial assets but also from the related advanced knowledge and expertise. Acquiring knowledge and production expertise from Germany is in line with China's 'Made in China 2025' strategy, which aims at the upgrading of manufacturing capabilities so as to meet China's goal of becoming a leading industrial nation by 2049. Other related reasons that have also contributed to Germany's popularity with Chinese investors include Germany's leading international position and competitiveness, the ability to open up access to other European markets, as well as the good reputation of the 'Made in Germany' label[404], something which is advantageous for attracting customers to buy finished products.

Related to these aims, the most important sectors for Chinese FDI in Germany have been automotive and industrial equipment. Between 2000 and 2014, automotive and industrial equipment accounted for more than 65% of total Chinese investment to the country[405]. Other important sectors have included renewable energy, consumer products and finance and transportation services. The majority of these investment in Germany take the form of acquisitions—according to one 2015 report this had accounted for 82% of Chinese FDI[406]—allowing for a quick way to enter the market and to acquire knowledge and assets. Nevertheless, Germany has lagged behind some European countries as a recipient of Chinese FDI in certain areas. These include the biggest sector for Chinese overseas investment in Europe, namely energy. Despite deals in renewable energy, overall investment is small in this sector when compared to other types of investments in energy (for instance energy extraction and utilities) in other European countries. Investment is also smaller in transportation, infrastructure, basic materials, metals and minerals[407].

The industrial regions of Germany are amongst those to receive the greatest proportion of Chinese FDI. Between 2000 and 2014, southern and western Germany (states of former West Germany) received the greatest amount of Chinese FDI. Bavaria, Hesse and North Rheine-Westphalia were the states that received the most, each receiving a cumulative value of FDI projects from Chinese companies in excess of one billion Euros[408].

Emerging concerns and cooling attitudes

Although still comparatively welcomed by the German government[409], concerns about the nature and consequences of Chinese investment in Germany have been growing. One of the major causes of this relates to fears over loss of technology and technological advantage. This has particularly been the case as the scale of investment has increased and coincided with China's stated ambition of catching up and competing with advanced manufacturing companies such as Germany. A Bertelsmann Stiftung foundation study found that between 2014 and 2017 almost two-thirds of China's mergers and acquisitions in Germany involved the ten sectors outlined in Beijing's 'Made in China 2025' plan[410]. It is not just the German government that is potentially concerned about this. According to one trade union consultant that we spoke to, while sometimes German trade unions viewed Chinese investment as being preferable to other types on investment, there was some fear about the future impact of technology transfer and the potentially resulting subsequent competition. Meanwhile, at the same time that Chinese FDI to Germany has been growing, German FDI to China has been declining in recent years[411].

The acquisition of German robotics manufacturer KUKA in 2016 by Chinese electrical appliance manufacturer Midea has been seen as a significant turning point in Chinese-German investment relations, causing concern from the government and workers alike. When the news was announced approximately 3,000 employees gathered at the Augsburg factory, worried about what the new ownership would mean for the company. However, two years later, according to the head of the Works Council at KUKA, Midea had committed to keeping the factories open and preserving jobs. The union IGMetall had also unsuccessfully sought to find alternative buyers for the company. Nevertheless, the acquisition also alarmed the government due to Kuka's position as a major company in a strategic sector of the economy. Indeed, the company has been described as, "a pioneer of Industry 4.0, the digitally networked economy"[412]. Although the government eventually conceded that the acquisition did not harm national interests, it did face opposition from some officials in Berlin and contributed to a political atmosphere in which the German government tightened regulations on all non-EU foreign investment in 2017[413]. Under the new regulations the government granted itself the power to intervene if a foreign company obtained a 25% stake or higher in a German company.

Examples of recent notable Chinese acquisitions in Germany

2011 Lenovo acquired a 51% stake for US$900 million in technology and consumer electronics company Medion.

2012 Weichai Power acquired a 25% stake in truck maker KION for 738 million euros. At the time it was China's largest direct investment in Germany.

2014 AVIC Systems (a subsidiary of aerospace and defence conglomerate AVIC) acquired automotive systems manufacturer Hilite International for 473 million euros.

2015 China's Zhongding Sealing Parts Co. Ltd acquired a 100% share in injection moulder company Wegu Holding GmbH for 95 million euros.

2016 China National Chemical Corporation (ChemChina) acquired a two-thirds stake in machinery manufacturer Kraus-Maffei for 925 million euros. At the time it was the largest Chinese acquisition of a German company.

2016 Beijing Enterprises Holding Limited acquired 100% of waste management company EEW Energy from Waste for 1.4 billion euros. The acquisition was agreed only a few weeks after the acquisition of Kraus-Maffei.

2016 investment group Fosun International Ltd. acquired 99.91% of equity interest in private bank Hauck & Aufhäuser for 210 million euros.

2017 Midea acquired a 94.55% stake in robot manufacturer Kuka for 4.5 billion euros.

2017 Biotest Pharmaceuticals agreed to a 1.3 billion takeover deal by China's Create Group Corp.

2017 China's HNA Group acquired a 700 million euros (3.04%) stake in Deutsche Bank AG. Later that year it was revealed that HNA's stake had risen to just under 10%.

2018 China's Geely Group acquired a 7.3 billion euros (9.7%) stake in Daimler – the biggest Chinese investment in a global automobile manufacturer to date.

In line with growing global trends, more recently there have been some additional signs that the German government has been growing warier of Chinese investment. In July 2018, Merkel's cabinet for the first time moved to veto the takeover of a German company by a Chinese company, when it signalled that it would block the acquisition of Leifeld Metal Spinning by Yantai Taihai group on "security grounds". Leifele Metal Spinning makes equipment for the nuclear energy and aerospace industries[414].

Exacerbated by the Chinese government's Made in China 2025 plan, the perceived political implications of Chinese investments are perhaps a related reason for the cooling attitudes towards it. This has particularly been so given the connection that many Chinese companies have to the Chinese state. This may not only include China's State-owned Enterprises (SOEs), which have been responsible for a significant proportion of China's overseas investment, but also companies with a sometimes unclear ownership structure, even where they claim a lack of connection. The growing global concern over the security of Huawei's technology and the way that the company is believed by many to be linked to the Chinese Communist Party (something that Huawei has denied) and the allegation that such technology could be used to spy for the Chinese government has not helped to improve this image. It should be noted that at the time of writing, however, Germany has not so far bowed to US pressure to ban Huawei[415]. Nevertheless, Chinese investments in small or medium sized German companies that specialise in advanced technology have sometimes been viewed more as political than economic acquisitions.

Restrictions have not just come from the German government, however. In 2017 the Chinese government also introduced new restrictions to regulate or restrict certain types of overseas investment by Chinese companies, partially in an attempt to limit capital flight. This led to a decline in Chinese ODI internationally and to some investors in restricted sectors, such as the hotel industry, withdrawing their investments. Following the introduction of new restrictions by China, German sellers have also reportedly sometimes been more cautious about Chinese investment and have asked for higher sums of money as collateral or other payment requirements that have contributed to the failure of some deals[416].

Investment in Manufacturing in North Rhine-Westphalia

View from the Alsumer Berg in Duisburg Marxloh: the North Rhine-Westphalia area was an early industrial centre. Photo Globalization Monitor.

In November 2018 we visited the industrial region of North Rhine-Westphalia, an area where a number of companies have been acquired by Chinese investors.

On our visit we met with representatives from works councils and trade unions associated with four companies that had been acquired by Chinese investors. We also learned about additional cases of Chinese investment in the region from other trade union researchers and consultants. All the companies were involved in manufacturing industries.

The Chinese companies that had acquired the four companies in Germany that we focused on had different ownership types. While Company A, Tailored Blanks, had been acquired by the State-Owned Enterprise (SOE) WISCO in 2013, which itself had subsequently been merged with central SOE, the Baosteel Group, in late 2016, two of the companies (Companies B and C) had been acquired by private mainland Chinese capital, one in 2010 and the other in 2014. The fourth company (Company D) had been recently acquired in 2017 by a Hong Kong company that had itself only recently been established in 2016. While Hong Kong capital is subject to different rules and different patterns of behaviour may be observed when compared to mainland Chinese capital, a significant proportion of 'Hong Kong' capital likely has its origins in the mainland[417]. Indeed, as far as Company D was concerned, on more closely examining the investing company's ownership structure and tracing it up to higher levels, it became evident that ultimately the Hong Kong company that had acquired Company D was very much connected to mainland Chinese capital. In addition, the chairperson of the investing company also held senior positions (chairperson and vice-chairperson respectively) in two mainland Chinese companies, which like Company D also produced equipment for the railway industry.

Outside the office of Chinese invested company WISCO tailored blanks in Duisburg. Photo: Globalization Monitor.

Acquisition

All four of the companies were experiencing some degree of financial difficulties at the time of acquisition and so the Chinese investment was largely, at least initially, viewed as something positive for securing the company's future by those we interviewed. In some cases, further investment in the company was promised for the future and so this was seen as a positive sign. For Company D, financial worries had been exacerbated due to China, which had been a major location for the sale of its products that were manufactured in Germany, changing its policy such that products produced in China were favoured over those from overseas. This had resulted in a loss of customers for the company. Acquisition by the Chinese company, which was linked to other companies producing for the Chinese market, was seen as a way to continue to access the Chinese market and improve the financial situation of the company. Experiences since the four companies were acquired by Chinese companies have varied, however. While some companies had experience layoffs, for others the further expected investment in the company had not always been forthcoming. In one case, concern was expressed that the financial system had changed and that the works council had little insight into the activities of the Chinese investor's holding company. Moreover, credits were being used to pay off old debts instead of for new investment as had been promised. Meanwhile some of the companies we visited or learned about had continued to experience losses and/or other financial difficulties since being acquired. In this respect, initial optimism and expectations had not been realized.

One complaint that emerged from one of the cases was that the acquisition process had taken much longer than had originally been hoped for. This was due to the long time needed for necessary permissions to be obtained in China for the Chinese company to acquire the German company. The degree of knowledge of the Chinese acquisition by worker representatives prior to the takeover seemed to vary, however. This was in part affected by the size of the company. Larger companies are entitled to greater representation, for instance the size of the company affects the number of works council members, and in companies where there are over 500 employees, workers are represented on a company's supervisory board and so may participate directly in decisions about the acquisition process. Regardless, works councils should be informed about the economic situation of the company and changes that could adversely impact the workforce[418].

Amongst the companies that we visited, one works council chairperson said that the works council had only become involved in negotiations around the acquisition after the workers had threatened to go on strike. At another company, works council members told us that they had learned about the potential acquisition when the Chinese investor company had sent a team of 40 to 50 people from China to the factories in Germany to carry out an investigation. At this company, the procedure was said to have taken about half a year, and, following the agreement of the sale of a majority stake in the company, an assembly was held to inform the company's employees, which involved a video call with the Chairperson from the investing group company. At Company D, as a company which at the time of acquisition had more than 500 employees, there was a trade union representative on the governing board of the company who was aware and involved during the acquisition process. Regardless of involvement in the process, however, other research has previously found that it is not uncommon for works councils and employees to have little contact with the new owners after a purchase has been completed, and this is something which has not sat well with employee representatives[419].

When companies in Germany are acquired by Chinese companies, it is common for agreements to be made protecting jobs and securing the location of the workplace lasting for five years. During this first period, relatively few changes are made by the Chinese investing company. After the five-year period, some changes were noticed by some of those we spoke to however, including adding more Chinese management and reducing the size of the workforce. At Company C it was noted that in the first five years, other than paying salaries, the Chinese company had largely left it alone and it did not invest a lot in machinery. Company B also had an agreement lasting five years protecting job security and was in the process of beginning to negotiate a new agreement. In one case, where a collective bargaining agreement for a 35 hour work week existed, it had been agreed to extend the work week by three hours with the same pay in exchange for guarantees of job security. At Company D, the most recently acquired of the companies, we were told that there had been some small-scale conflicts over reducing costs and the arrangement of shifts and rest time, but the trade union representative seemed keen to point out that this type of conflict was not unique to the period since there had been Chinese investment.

Workforce reductions

A number of the Chinese invested companies in the region had continued to experience significant losses and had started to cut the number of workers. Tailored Blanks was one such example. It had begun a layoff program with the aim of cutting 50 of its 270 workers and had begun to negotiate conditions with the works council from March 2018. According to Deniz Erdogan the Works Council Chairperson, the management did not initially understand that it had to negotiate with the works council or that it would have to pay compensation for laying people off. Two weeks before our meeting with him in mid-November, an agreement on the redundancies had been signed over the amount of compensation. There would be 40 voluntary redundancies, while the workforce would be reduced by a further 10 as a result of the expiration of existing contracts. The amount of compensation agreed seemed to be very appealing to workers. As a result, 60 workers had volunteered for the redundancy even though they had only needed to find 40 workers to volunteer. We were told that the total cost for reducing the number of employees would be around 5 million euros, and that the money for this would come from Baosteel, the Chinese owner, directly. An additional condition was that there would be no more layoffs in 2019. Interestingly, according to the works council chairperson, the company had previously been presented to them as a big company with lots of money that never laid people off. Baosteel is one of the world's biggest steel producers and in 2017 was ranked by the World Steel Association as the second largest steel producer in the world in terms of volume[420].

Company	No. Employees in Nov. 2018	Redundancies and workforce reductions
Company A	270	The company was preparing to reduce the workforce by 50 workers.
Company B	350 (280 permanent and 70 contract workers)	
Company C	200	Técnicas Reunidas S.A., Hanwha Engineering &Construction, KNPC
Company D	480	Técnicas Reunidas S.A., Hanwha Engineering &Construction, KNPC

Tailored Blanks was not the only case that we heard about in the region where the workforce had been downsized or faced that prospect in the near future. Company C had also faced significant job losses since being acquired by a Chinese company. This company had 700 employees at the time of its acquisition by the Chinese investor in 2010. In 2015 the number of employees was reduced to 350 and in 2017 to just 200. One of the main threats to employment at this factory was the relocation of production. Due to the cheaper costs, the company was moving manufacturing to its factory in Serbia and had been sending machinery and equipment from this factory there. When we looked around the factory, we saw large empty spaces where there was once machinery. Amongst remaining machinery, there were additional items already packed up and ready to send. We were told by a works council member that the company seemed to intend to make the components in Serbia and then assemble them in Germany so that the "made in Germany" label could still be used. He believed, however, that the ultimate aim was to produce everything in China. Five years after acquiring the company, copies of everything at the factory had been made and sent to China. The Chinese company had then started to produce some motors in China, although the quality was described as being "different" to those produced in Germany. The same fate (concerning employment and the relocation of production) was said to be facing the company's other two German factories.

Company D had also experienced a reduction of its workforce. At the time of the sale to the Hong Kong company there had been 594 employees, but when we visited Germany in November 2018 this had fallen to 480. The trade union representative that we spoke to about this case did not attribute the workforce reduction to the Chinese investment. Accordingly, there had already been plans in place to reduce the workforce by 120 in order to level out company losses. The workforce had been reduced through not replacing workers who retired due to old age and through voluntary redundancies.

During our visit, we also heard about difficulties at engineering company KHD Humboldt WEDAG following its acquisition. A 90% stake in the company, which provides products and services to the cement industry, was acquired by Chinese SOE AVIC International Beijing Co. Ltd, a member unit of the central aerospace and defence SOE the Aviation Industry Corporation of China (AVIC Group), in 2011. In discussing the current situation, the company was described by a trade union consultant that we spoke with as facing a critical situation, lacking new strategy from China and having made losses in the last couple of years. Having already reduced the workforce by 19%, on 12th March 2019, the company announced that Humboldt Wedag, a major subsidiary of KHD Humboldt Wedag based in Cologne, was planning to cut approximately 80 jobs and that it would be discussing this with the works council in the coming weeks[421].

The experiences that we heard about during our fieldwork in Germany and from local media reports, where despite the initial positive expectations of the investment the workforce was subsequently reduce, are consistent with a recent study published by the Hans Bockler Foundation that records 14 cases of high job losses at Chinese invested companies, the majority (12) of which has been acquired between 2011 and 2013. Two of these cases involved 100% of the workforce being cut as the companies became insolvent[422].

Changes and new challenges encountered

While as a recent acquisition it was too early to tell concerning the company acquired by the Hong Kong investor, at the other three companies, although relatively little changed immediately following acquisition, after a period of time some changes had occurred. One of the major changes was to the management. Although initially management mostly stayed the same, over time Chinese managers were brought in, either alongside or replacing German management. Not all of the Chinese managers could speak German. Even where companies retained some German management, one additional problem was that there was no direct line of communication with those responsible for decision making in China. One works council chairperson said that it, "is nearly impossible to deal with them", and that any decisions took months to come back from China. He told us that there was very little information about what was getting reported back to China and he suspected that the Chinese management were not reporting anything back about what had been discussed with them.

"Cultural differences" and relevant knowledge of how things worked in Germany were also identified as a big problem. Translation problems were one issue that was highlighted, however a lack of understanding of procedures, how meetings were run, democratic decision making as well as inadequate understanding of the German legal system and its protection of workers' rights were also reported. One works council chairperson commented on his impression that if a company is doing badly the Chinese management just expect the workers to take a pay cut. He commented that even if this might be normal in China, it is not in Germany. Some interviewees noted the Chinese managers' concern about losing face in China when they encountered difficulties in running the company in Germany. One of the Chinese companies had also run into problems when it had started to renovate a building only for it to be discovered that it had not sought relevant planning permissions. The building in question was standing vacant and unused when we visited.

While one of the aims of Chinese companies investing in Germany is to obtain access to European markets, this has not always been a straightforward process. Overconfidence or lack of experience by the Chinese investing company have resulted in some difficulties. This has included inexperience on the part of the Chinese investors in selling to relevant customers. In the case of Wisco and Tailored Blanks, for instance, while the original intention was for Tailored Blanks to use Wisco's steel in its manufacturing following the acquisition, Wisco's steel was reportedly not good enough to use in Germany's auto industry and this had meant it had to buy steel from other companies, contributing to financial losses. Fortunately for this case, following Wisco's merger with Baosteel, Baosteel had been able to send over good quality suitable steel and so there was more room for optimism about the future. Indeed, the works council chairperson believed that if Baosteel had not taken over then the company would have had to close; instead they would now have the chance to be more competitive. A lack of familiarity with the European market was also identified as being a problem at Company C. Although everything at the factory in Germany was custom made, the Chinese investing company was used to producing serial models and had little understanding of the scales involved. This was said to have led to the loss of a lot of customers.

Other than the reduction of the workforce and some additional pressure from the management, working conditions at the factories were said to have changed very little if at all at the companies that we visited since they had been acquired by Chinese investors. Nevertheless, it was observed that some of the Chinese investors were more concerned about profit margins than the previous owners had been. Works council members at Company B, for instance, commented that the new investors had expected higher profit margins, however, due to an increase in the secondary costs of production such as energy prices, its profits had fallen, and so this was experienced as a pressure for the works council.

At one of the workplaces, the company had previously sent a small number (10 to 20) workers from China to Germany to work on the production line, however this stopped when it was discovered that the workers only had tourist visas (and so did not have permission to work in Germany). These workers had been accompanied by a translator, but it was nonetheless still unclear to the works council whether they had been properly introduced to the relevant safety procedures at the factory.

Machinery for mining produced by Schorch on display at the Zollern colliery museum in Dortmund.

The company has a long history dating back to the nineteenth century. It was acquired by the Chinese Wolong Group in 2010. Photo: Globalization Monitor.

Future prospects

Overall, there were different degrees of optimism concerning the future of work at the four companies that we visited. At Company C, with the workforce significantly reduced and machinery and production increasingly being shifted elsewhere, the outlook seemed bleak; at the other companies there was still a higher degree of optimism remaining.

Works council members from Company B, for instance, said that they felt relatively positive about the future. They expressed the hope that the holding group company would buy up more companies that could make use of the products that they produced, thereby helping to safeguard work. According to a representative from the local trade union that we spoke to about Company D, workers at this company were initially worried about the takeover and what would happen in 5 to 6 years' time. Nevertheless, he claimed that although there are a lot of changes going on in the industry as well as big competition, for now, thanks to the Chinese investment the company was relatively stable.

Duisburg – China's 'Gateway to Europe'?

Interested by all the media hype around the new role of Duisburg and its significance to China, we also visited this city and the railway container terminal for the route originating in China. The city of Duisburg, a steel and coal town for much of the twentieth century, was already considered the world's largest inland port before Beijing's plans to revive the Silk Road. Now, with the China Railway Express railway service linking Duisburg to China, the port is reportedly fast becoming one of Europe's central logistics hubs. For China, it marks a very important strategic location in its Belt and Road initiative as the Western terminus of the new Silk Road. The route from Chongqing to Duisburg, which was first launched in 2011, with regular cargo trains travelling between the two cities since 2015, covers more than 10,000 kilometres, passing through Xinjiang, Kazakhstan, Russia, Belarus and Poland. The train runs to the river Rhine arriving at the Duisburg Intermodal Terminal (DIT), where the goods can then be loaded onto ships.

According to reports, it is the first stop of about 80% of trains from mainland China and around 25 to 30 trains arrive at Duisburg's inland port from China every week[423]. Last year DIT reportedly leased an additional 200,000 square metres of land from Duisburg port due to growing Chinese business[424]. According to the port's CEO, Erich Staake, freight sent by rail between Chongqing and Duisburg costs almost twice as much as shipping it, however it is much faster and only takes 12 instead of 45 days. However, in terms of cargo volume, trade is not equally balanced or beneficial for the German side. Only half the number of full containers return to China as those that arrive in Duisburg from China, and the port only earns a fifth of the fee for empty containers sent back to China[425].

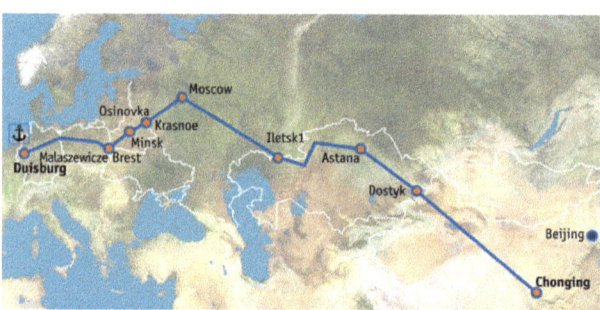

The rail route between Chongqing and Duisburg. Source: Belarusian Railway.

A China Railway Container Transport Corp. Ltd. (CRCT) container on a train at the terminal in Duisburg. Photo: Globalization Monitor.

Duisburg is a city with high unemployment, standing at 12% in 2018, a rate almost four times the national average. With this in mind, the rail link has been presented as beneficial to the city for its potential to create employment. Indeed, since the rail link first began operation, additional drivers and workers have been hired to deal with the increased container transportation. A 2018 Xinhua report cites Duisburg's city official for Chinese affairs, Johannes Pflug, as claiming that the rail transport business from this has created over 6,000 jobs[426]. This is something which may continue as additional land is purchased for warehouses and a logistics centre connected to the rail link, although we were told by a local activist that the plan was to construct this some distance from Duisburg and so potential benefits to the city might be questionable. At the same time, there has also been some impact for Chinese business in the city. Since Xi Jinping visited Duisburg in 2014 on his state visit to Germany, the number of Chinese businesses in the city have reportedly doubled since to 100 companies. With the potential prospects for new business and to gain further market access, there are also plans for Chinese developer, the Starhai Group, to build a 260 million Euro 'China Trade Centre Europe' in at the Niederrhein Business Park in Duisburg[427].

Nevertheless, despite the presentation of the rail link's significance in both Western and Chinese media, other than job creation, the idea that the rail link might have much significant impact for the city was met with a certain degree of scepticism by some local activists, who did not see it as such an important issue for the city. In speaking about Chinese investment in the city more generally, one activist did raise concern about data security and the city's planned partnership with Huawei over digitalization. In January 2018, Duisburg and Huawei had signed a Memorandum of Understanding to work together on 'smart city' development. Unlike in some countries where China has invested, however, Chinese investment in the city was described as something that was accepted and not something that was a cause of conflict or opposition. Indeed, in contrast to some other cities along the New Silk Road, the port remains German run[428]. The independence of the city is something that local officials are reportedly keen to maintain. Aware of the fate of Sri Lankan Hambantota Port, Chinese affairs official Johannes Pflug has said that, "we must preserve our independence and at all costs avoid falling into a debt trap with the Chinese"[429].

A China Shipping container on a train at the terminal in Duisburg. Photo: Globalization Monitor.

The Hamburg Port Investment Plan

A China Shipping container on a train at the terminal in Duisburg. Photo: Globalization Monitor.

In Hamburg a very different story appears to be unfolding. Proposed plans for Chinese companies to develop part of the port there are a significant cause for concern according to local activists and works council representatives.

Hamburg port is the largest port in Germany and the third largest in Europe. Handling 8.9 million TEUs of containers in 2016, it ranked 17th globally in terms of the volume of container throughput[430]. It is therefore a significant location for trade and logistics. Hamburg Port already has four major existing container terminals: Container Terminal Altenwerder, Container Terminal Burchardkai, Container Terminal Tollerort and EUROGATE Container Terminal. Apart from the EUROGATE terminal, the other three terminals are operated by Hamburger Hafen und Logistik AG (HHLA), a logistics and transportation company that the state of Hamburg has retained a 68.4% stake in[431], after it was partially privatized and made an IPO on the Frankfurt Stock Exchange in 2007. Container Terminal Altenwerder is considered 'state-of-the-art'[432] and is notable for its high degree of automation.

Despite its significance in Europe and globally as a major transportation and logistics hub, Hamburg port has been shrinking in size, both in terms of land used for port activities and the volume of cargo handled. As a result, some of the port area has been given over to real estate. This includes land for the development of Hafen City – a 157 hectare area of decommissioned harbour space that is expected to have 12,000 residents by 2025[433]. The number of containers handled has also been declining especially since 2008 and it has begun to lose some ground to other ports such as Antwerp and Rotterdam.

Nevertheless, in response to declining throughput at the port of Hamburg in the first quarter of 2018, it was noted that a growth in container traffic with some countries nevertheless occurred. China was one of these countries. According to Ingo Egloff, Joint CEO of Port of Hamburg Marketing:

China is by a wide margin the Port of Hamburg's most important trading partner. We can report a distinct advance of 4.5 percent in container traffic with the Peoples' Republic. Substantial growth also occurred on container services with Brazil (up 37.7 percent), Sweden (up 38.5 percent) and Israel (up 63.8 percent). New or expanded liner services between Hamburg and these countries are one reason for the positive trend.[434].

New Development Plans

Even though the port has been experiencing a decline, in January 2017 the Hamburg Port Authority opened a five month initial ideas competition to develop Steinwerder-Süd, a 42 hectare area of the port. Later that year, Shanghai Zhenhua Port Machinery (ZPMC) Germany GmbH and its parent Chinese multinational engineering and construction company China Communications Construction Company Ltd. (CCCC)[435] were declared the winner of the competition with a proposal to build a new fully automated container terminal. The potential construction costs are estimated to be between 1.2 and 1.4 billion euros. According to one interviewee from a port related works council, the Chinese bid was unusual as for the first time it proposed to "include everything", "both the superstructure and infrastructure". This would mean that CCCC would be responsible for all of the construction work thereby gaining greater control over the constructed terminal and its operation. In previous practice, the city itself would have been responsible for providing and maintaining the infrastructure. Second place in the competition reportedly went to a plan to develop a shortsea terminal at the site by Dutch company the C Steinweg Group[436]. The City of Hamburg had also put in an unsuccessful bid for the development of the port area.

The plans by CCCC to construct the new terminal have been met with criticism from existing businesses at the port, which claim that there is insufficient business at the port for an additional terminal that would only result in the redistribution of existing business leading to job instability[437], and port related works council members who also said that it will adversely impact on jobs. Indeed, the Hamburg Port Authority's own development plan had estimated that the existing terminals and their projected expansion could cope with forecasted volumes up until at least 2025[438]. The reasons for declaring the CCCC project the winner have been questioned.

Representatives from all three of the works councils that we spoke with in relation to the port expressed scepticism about the need for a new container terminal, especially in light of the fact that the existing terminals are not currently operating to full capacity and the decline in the volume of containers that the port has been handling since 2008. One estimate suggested that the port has the capacity to deal with an additional 5 million TEU above what it currently handles. According to Hamburg Port Authority works council chair, Doris Heinemann-Brooks, since the 2008 crisis there has been so little capacity that cranes have simply remained parked. They have not yet been successful at getting the cargo to return to the port. Some of it now goes to Poland and Rotterdam and possibly Croatia, as labour is deemed cheaper and faster elsewhere in Europe. While Cargo has been lost from the port, so far there has been little impact on jobs, although there have been some cuts and short time work in the past two years. Concern was expressed about potential salary reductions in the future, something that increased competition, for instance as a result of the proposed new terminal might exacerbate. Another works council chair estimated that plans for the new terminal would cost a couple of hundred jobs, both through intensification of competition and the fact that the proposed new terminal would be fully automated. Meanwhile HHLA Works Council chairperson, Norbert Paulsen, estimated that the plans could cost as many as 400 jobs.

For jobs that were not expected to be cut, the perceived potential threat to labour rights and to jobs that paid well was another issue worrying the works councils. Specifically referencing cases of poor working conditions in Chinese invested workplaces elsewhere in Europe, such as in textiles in the Italian region of Tuscany as well as problems at the Port of Piraeus in Greece, one interviewee expressed concern that similar problems could occur in Hamburg. Indeed, prompted by concerns around the experiences of Chinese investment elsewhere, German activists had already begun to have exchanges about their experiences with trade union activists in Greece, who had been affected by Chinese state-owned shipping and logistics company COSCO's investment in the port of Piraeus.

The proposed site for the new container terminal in Hamburg. Photo: Globalization Monitor.

In the Hamburg case, while at the time of our visit plans for the Chinese investment were still not finalized, the circumstances related to the competition and development plans for the construction of the new terminal were considered unusual and a break with past decisions. One reason was that the whole process around the plans were considered undemocratic and lacking in transparency. One works council member noted that while there was a long tradition of democratic discussions, experiences so far with this plan differed. He labelled it an "outrageous coup d'état" to give away such an important piece of the port without a democratic process. He also commented that there was a rumour that some sort of secret deal might have been done during the G20 summit the previous year. Regardless of whether or not there is any degree of truth behind such a rumour, the very existence of such a rumour is a reflection on the lack of trust in decision making procedures concerning the development plans.

Significantly, the plans to develop the port also coincided with changes to the length of land leases. Whereas previously port land could only be leased for 40 years, following the competition the maximum length for a possible lease was changed to 99 years. According to those we interviewed, the parliament passed this change to the law with little discussion. The fact that whoever eventually was given the go-ahead to develop the area might be able to do whatever they wanted to with it, for instance to close access to it or to import workers, was also viewed as alarming.

Indeed, another factor that was deemed unusual about development plans was that it did not provide room for money from the use of the land to flow back to the city to benefit the public, as by giving up the land in this way the state would lose a potential source of revenue. Such investment was viewed as problematic, regardless of the country where the investor came from. One explanation for the change in approach was the political and economic situation in Hamburg and behaviour of the banks. Accordingly, the large amount of money lost through speculation was believed to have led to a situation where the city lacked money to invest in the port itself.

At the same time, while the procedures and plans for the potential new developments were considered alarming due to the potential for it to set a precedent for other investment to follow in a similar manner (threatening labour rights and eroding democracy), concerns were also raised about the negative impact that privatization had already had elsewhere. Meanwhile, the problem of lack of space and a lack of affordable housing in Hamburg was contrasted with the proposal to develop an unnecessary additional container terminal.

Despite these concerns, it was noted that the local trade unions were largely unopposed to the plans for the port due to their traditional ties to the social democrats who supported the proposed development. This was viewed as a factor that made it more difficult to challenge the plans. There had been some small-scale opposition both

The Hamburg Port Authority. Photo: Globalization Monitor.

in the local parliament and attempts outside the parliament to inform the general public; however what was perceived by interviewees as a lack of interest in labour matters had, they believed, meant that it had so far been difficult to attract more widespread attention to challenge problematic aspects of the development plan. It was hoped that in the future they would be able to find a way to inform the public and create resistance, such as by holding a big public demonstration to display the strength of the opposition to the plans.

We also learned that a new law which is expected to change the management of the Hamburg Port Authority was under preparation and was expected to be ready by summer 2019. This was considered alarming in light of the plans to develop the port, however little was so far known about the details.

Another existing container terminal in Hamburg. This container terminal is automated. Photo: Globalization Monitor.

Exploring Chinese investment in Germany

While this preliminary exploration that draws on our visit to Germany in November

2018 is not an in-depth study and is only able to consider some of the issues stemming from a small number of examples, it does begin to give an indication of some patterns emerging concerning Chinese investment and identifies challenges being faced by some Chinese invested companies in Germany, amongst which are issues that are a cause for concern. Such issues include a lack of understanding of local laws and procedures by the investors, an inability by the investor to fully grasp the operations of the company and/or customers, communication difficulties and cultural differences, a potential threat to labour rights, and a lack of transparency and erosion of democratic decision-making processes. Moreover, while investments may at first appear to offer solutions to financial difficulties and protect jobs, in some cases this seems to have faced limits and subsequent changes in behaviour and management on the part of the investor may occur after only a few years. The long-term intentions and plans of investors may also be unknown. While earlier research by Bian and Emons concluded that, despite some negative impacts, Chinese investment had so far been more positive than originally feared, our own preliminary research suggests a need for caution when considering the long-term impacts.

Learning about experiences elsewhere, as labour activists in Hamburg and Greece have been trying to do, is one way to gain greater awareness and become better prepared for any potential challenges that similar types of investment might bring. Although Chinese investments in some developing countries have increasingly been criticized for their potential adverse impacts on labour, local people and the environment amongst other issues, investments in Western countries such as Germany have sometimes been viewed as comparatively less problematic. The experiences that we learned about on our visit to Germany suggest that this is not something that should be so readily assumed. That is not to say that issues faced are necessarily the same—investments and how they are viewed and experienced as well as their impacts are often greatly affected by the economic and political situation of the countries concerned—however comparing and sharing experiences may be greatly beneficial to those who are affected.

Part 9: Where does it lead? Challenges for Chinese Overseas Investment and the Belt and Road Initiative

In October 2017, just two years after it was launched, Xi Jinping's Belt and Road Initiative was given a further political boost when it was written into the Communist Party constitution, thereby signaling that officials should pay even greater attention to this vision. Although clearly important to the Chinese party state's goals and ambitions, it is nevertheless worth asking what this road has meant in practice and where it really leads.

Indeed, despite both its drawing on the historical legacy of the ancient Silk Road and also having been presented as an ambitious new initiative for the twenty-first century and the "new era", beyond highlighting geographic regions and broadly outlining areas of focus, specific details about what is to be newly included might be deemed a little bit vague. Moreover, with plans for many of the major projects that are now included in the BRI having been devised or already initiated prior to the BRI first being announced and some projects, such as CPEC, dating back decades and later incorporated into the initiative, it is hard to see the BRI as something completely new. It is nevertheless true that the BRI era has seen extra focus and additional money (albeit at a slower rate than might have initially been expected) prioritized for investments in BRI regions, as well as the signing of Memorandum of Understanding (MOU) for cooperation between China and BRI countries[439], although these MOUs do not guarantee substantive actions take place. With this in mind, in many senses the BRI might be viewed as simply the continuation or next stage in the advancement of processes and agendas dating back several decades, and as a "marketing" or promotional strategy to illustrate China's vision and encourage other countries to get on board and sign up to China's political and economic goals globally.

While the BRI and Chinese overseas investments strategies are clearly designed to be advantageous to China itself, China has been keen to present the initiative as offering benefits to recipient countries claiming that BRI opportunities represent "win-win" situations. Indeed, as far as Chinese investment has been viewed as politically and economically advantageous to their own interests, overseas governments and political leaders have often welcomed the investment opportunities, and even sometimes drawn on the BRI to affirm their own vision or that of the country's own historical legacy. Iran is one such example, presenting the new Silk Road as representative of its own cultural and historical ties with neighbouring countries[440].

But are such wins guaranteed? The BRI and other Chinese investments have frequently run into significant problems. Indeed, Chinese officials themselves early recognized that 80% of money invested in Pakistan, half of that invested in Myanmar and a third in Central Asia will most likely be lost[441]. However as noted in Part 7, although making a profit is an important for many investing companies, it might not always have been the most immediate concern for some projects or investments. While profit is certainly a major aim of Chinese overseas investment (including that of major state-owned companies), building up influence for longer term economic (for instance to gain market access or more advanced technological knowledge) and political (for instance to win over friends, limit the influence of rivals or to establish regional hegemony) power may sometimes be a greater factor. At the same time, there is a lot of evidence that Chinese investments often do not constitute a "win-win", either for local governments or for ordinary people in the countries concerned. Problematic areas have included treatment of local people, workers (local and Chinese) and the environment; corruption; high costs and debt; as well as exacerbated geopolitical tensions. This has led to some changing and negative attitudes towards Chinese investments. Subsequently, many projects have experienced delays or cancellations, due to mounting costs, changing political agendas or local resistance, while some projects simply do not appear to have been economically viable in the first place. With the onset of the Covid-19 pandemic, many BRI projects now face additional setbacks. The following sections summarise some of the major problems associated with the BRI and Chinese overseas investment and then considers some strategies and recommendations for limiting adverse outcomes.

Labour

Despite the Chinese government having issued a number of non-binding guidelines for Chinese companies operating overseas to encourage better practice and adherence to local laws, mechanisms to enforce them are lacking and labour rights violations, poor working conditions and even the driving down of existing standards and job losses (for instance following the COSCO acquisition at the Port of Piraeus in Greece) occur at many overseas Chinese invested workplaces.

While poor labour standards are by no means unique to Chinese investment, there is one additional challenge for building solidarity to resist Chinese capital overseas and to seek labour rights improvements for workers at Chinese invested companies: international trade unions and trade unions in the countries concerned cannot draw on support from affiliates in China as they might attempt to do in challenging multinational capital from other countries. In China independent trade unions are prohibited and the All-China Federation of Trade Unions (ACFTU) is the only institution legally recognized to act as a trade union. This is especially problematic since it is an organ of the party-state mandated to pursue China's development interests as set out by the Chinese Communist Party (including those related to Chinese state capital). Domestically, it is widely acknowledged that the ACFTU does not prioritise the protection of the rights of Chinese workers in China, who will often bypass it when they need to take action to protect their interest. Internationally, the ACFTU has no international affiliation and although it has, sometimes aggressively, pursued contact and relations with overseas unions, the forms that this has the potential to take are severely restricted by the aims of the CCP.

While some have suggested that in cases of Chinese investment overseas, trade unions attempt to establish contact with the ACFTU[442], there is therefore a lot of reason to be skeptical about the potential for this to act as a meaningful basis for international solidarity aimed at protecting the rights of workers in both countries. On the contrary a case might be made that giving legitimacy to the ACFTU in this is harmful to the interests of workers in China. Indeed, the lack of freedom of association in China is one major reason to be concerned about the (rapid) expansion of China's overseas investments in recent years and poses a great challenge for the labour movement internationally.

Meanwhile, perhaps contrary to its official stance of non-interference in the affairs of other countries, Chinese state media has at times advocated for limiting the influence of overseas unions so as to maintain an attractive environment for Chinese investors. In February 2017, following strike action by local workers in Myanmar against a Chinese invested garment factory, reportedly due to the company's dismissal and refusal to rehire a local trade union leader and for the renegotiation of company bonus rules, an article in Chinese party-state newspaper the Global Times argued that it was necessary for Myanmar to, "restrict the power of local labor unions according to relevant laws to better protect foreign investors' legitimate rights". The article observed that Chinese companies lack experience in how to deal with its unions, and commented that, "The immoderate use of labour unions to improve worker's welfare or seek interests for union members is likely to hurt foreign investors' enthusiasm, especially in increasing investment in labor-intensive manufacturing sectors"[443].

Another major issue specifically concerning labour and Chinese overseas investment is the use of imported rather than local labour. Even though there is evidence suggesting that its use may be declining in some countries, when Chinese companies are awarded construction and other contracts overseas, it is still not uncommon for them to import Chinese workers to work on these projects. Perceived lack of job creation for local workers, differing treatments concerning wages and benefits, as well as language and cultural misunderstandings have sometimes led to tensions and anti-Chinese sentiments. Nevertheless, many overseas Chinese workers have also been victims of exploitation and rights violations at the hands of Chinese contracted or investing companies as well as labour dispatch employment agencies. Unpaid wages and visa issues have been amongst problems that they have faced. In

2017, for instance, Malaysian media reported that Chinese migrant workers working on the construction of the Forest City project in Malaysia were facing wage arrears and had not been provided with the proper work visas after being cheated by agents in China to whom they needed to repay huge loans[444]. Another example involves the use of undocumented Chinese construction workers in Saipan, who were hired to work on projects contracted to Chinese companies constructing the Imperial Palace Casino. After having paid at least 10,000 Yuan each to labour agencies in China to obtain their posts, many of the workers had to work long hours in violation of local labour laws, were paid below the local minimum wage and faced high occupational injury rates. In this case the workers fought back and won some compensation for unpaid wages after a US$14 million settlement was agreed between the Chinese companies and the US department of labour in 2018, although some workers it was reported not to have been enough to pay off debts resulting from payment of recruitment agencies in China[445].

Environmental Costs

Chinese overseas investment has also been a cause for concern due to environmental issues such as pollution, destruction of habitats and natural resource depletion, as well as impacts to the livelihoods and homes of local people due to land use or displacement. This is despite the Chinese government repeatedly stating its commitment to environmentally sustainable investment and advancing clean energy when outlining its plans for the BRI and overseas investments. For instance, in reporting on China's proposed 3 marine passages for the BRI, the China Daily notes that:

The Chinese government called on nations participating in the 21st Century Maritime Silk Road to work together to preserve marine ecology, boost maritime connectivity, foster marine economy, safeguard security at sea, deepen research in oceanography and enhance collaboration, according to the document.

To achieve these goals, China plans to carry out a host of measures, such as establishing a marine environmental protection cooperation mechanism with the Association of Southeast Asian Nations; supporting island nations coping with climate change and ocean disasters; and sharing research capability with partners[446]*.*

The Chinese government has also issued guidelines and regulations (again non-binding and difficult to enforce) that apply to issues related to environmental protection, including, for instance, the Guidelines for Environmental Protection in Foreign Investment and Cooperation, issued in 2013. Nevertheless, overseas infrastructure projects and the activities of many companies continue to harm the environment, sometimes in violation of local legislation. In 2019, for instance, inspections at 32 gold mining sites in northern Congo revealed that the Chinese company, Agil Congo, a company which did not have a mining permit, had destroyed 150 streams while prospecting for gold[447]. The US$62 billion CPEC has also come under significant criticism due to potential adverse environmental impacts, with the destruction of farmlands, forests, a strain on natural resources and some negative impacts on livelihoods reported[448]. Indeed, BRI projects often require a large amount of land for the construction of infrastructure and the development of industrial zones have sometimes resulted in land being grabbed from local populations, resulting in families being displaced and livelihoods lost. In Laos, for instance, the construction of the China-Laos railway reportedly replaced 4,411 families with very few of them having been compensated in accordance with local regulations[449]. Meanwhile, plans for Malaysia's East Coast Rail Link, which was intended to be completed by 2026, have been criticized for risks posed to biological diversity through its disruption of the habitats of peatlands, estuaries, mangroves, lagoons[450]. In some cases, for instance involving dams on the Mekong River, Chinese invested projects have been implemented without adequate Environmental Impact Assessment approvals[451].

This is all especially worrying since along planned BRI economic corridors there are an estimated 91,222 protected areas that may be affected by its projects, as well as 265 threatened, endangered or critically endangered species[452]. While Chinese companies have frequently faced fines for environmental damage, this means very little in an area where the harm done could potentially be long-term or irreversible.

One particular area of concern regarding the long-term environmental consequences of Chinese investment relates to the expansion of investment in non-renewable energy sources. Despite commitments to renewable energies, in the official NDRC Vision and Action plan for the BRI, "the exploration and development of coal, oil, gas, metal minerals and other conventional energy sources" is highlighted as an area for increased cooperation[453]. These are energy sources which are known to necessarily have significant adverse environmental impacts, contributing to global warming. Between 2001 and 2016, China was involved in 240 coal power projects in countries that it now classifies as part of the BRI. India, Indonesia, Mongolia, Vietnam and Turkey were the top five countries in which it was involved[454]. This commitment not only impacts countries where China is involved in building coal power plants and other energy related infrastructure, the supply of fossil fuels such as oil and gas to China has been something that BRI projects have sought to secure or further develop. Such is the significance of this type of energy for Chinese overseas investment that, as of 2017 Russia had been the largest recipient country of Chinese overseas financing (OOF and ODA), largely as a result of a US$25 billion loan package provided by China Development Bank in 2009 to oil company Rosneft and pipeline builder Transneft. A further US$6 million was provided to Russia in loans-for-coal in 2010[455]. Meanwhile, with Saudi Arabia now also invited to join CPEC, there are plans to turn Gwadar Port into a petroleum city, with US$10 billion of Saudi funding[456].

Corruption

Like companies from many other countries, Chinese companies have been frequently accused of corruption related to their overseas activities. Nevertheless, the scale of the lack of transparency and corruption related to some Chinese companies is particularly notable. Indeed, in a 2016 survey by Transparency International of 100 companies based in emerging market economies, Chinese companies ranked worst overall and 9 of the worst ranking 10 companies were Chinese[457]. The fact that the China Communications Construction Company (CCCC) and its subsidiaries have had so many allegations of corruption made against them related to overseas activities (see Part 5), yet the group still represents one of the leading contractors for BRI infrastructure construction projects, is in itself alarming. While corruption may help with the procurement of contracts and other business agreements or line the pockets of various (local or Chinese) officials, it may also harm local people, workers and the environment when regulations that protect them are overlooked or resources diverted away from places where there might be greater need. Despite repeated pledges by China to tackle corruption in BRI countries and China's anti-graft body, the Central Commission for Discipline Inspection, reportedly planning to embed officers in BRI countries for the first time[458], widespread significant progress remains to be seen.

Debt

With Chinese banks making huge loans to developing countries often to finance infrastructure and other mega-construction projects, the (lack of) sustainability of the projects and the question of whether the countries taking out the loans really have the ability to repay or whether they will be left with unsustainable debt problems is a cause for concern. Pakistan, Kyrgyzstan, Mongolia and Laos, Maldives, Djibouti, Montenegro, Tajikistan and Mongolia have been identified as facing significant debt stress, with a potential to have to default if further loans are made.

In some cases, Chinese loans may carry increased risks and high interest rates. For recipient countries, since loans are mostly denominated in dollars or RMB, borrowers are also potentially susceptible to risks form changing exchange rates. These are therefore factors that may increase debt burdens. In other countries, for instance in some African countries, as well as Brazil, Ecuador, Venezuela and Russia, China has signed resource backed loan agreements, such as oil-for-loans agreements, whereby Chinese banks offer loans guaranteed by oil shipments. This arrangement has meant that the banks can afford to make the loans at lower rates than US and European banks that are bound by OECD rules[459]. Nevertheless, these too can carry great risks for the countries concerned, especially so when the oil price crashes, as cases such as Angola and Venezuela have shown.

Sri Lanka's leasing out of the Hambantota port to China for 99 years in the face of the former country's debt to China and other international lenders has been the most widely cited example invoking fears around the consequences of racking up significant debt and the potential for Chinese loans to contribute to a 'debt trap' for less well-off countries. In this case, the debt (borrowed mostly at commercial rates to a country already very much in debt) owed to China's Exim bank for the construction of another (perhaps unnecessary) port for the country was not cancelled with the lease and still needs to be repaid. However, the US$1.12 billion paid to Sri Lanka for the lease was used to strengthen Sri Lanka's dollar reserves in 2017-2018 in light of its huge external debt servicing[460].

Since the Sri Lankan port case, there has been widespread international fear that other countries will be forced to cede similar assets if they are unable to service their debts, especially in the face of mounting debts to China. In 2018, drawing comparisons to Sri Lanka, concerns surfaced that Kenya would have to give up its Mombasa port after it was reportedly offered as collateral for underperforming loans[461]. Chinese and Kenyan authorities denied the situation[462]. The Sri Lanka case was also cited by trade unionists and works council members working at both the Hamburg Port in Germany and Pireaus Port in Greece, who Globalization Monitor interviewed in November 2018. Meanwhile in 2018, Tonga Prime Minister Samiuela Akilisi Pohiv expressed fear about the potential seizure of strategic assets in the face of the country's debt of US$115 million to China. As one of eight islands in the South Pacific with significant debt to China he expressed how he thought that the region should negotiate collectively: "It is no longer an issue for individual countries because there are small countries who borrowed from China and we have problems with that and the option is to collectively work together to find a way out."[463] However, later that year in October 2018, the nation joined the BRI and was granted a five year reprieve on the repayment of its debts by China[464]. Signing up to China's grand plan coincided with debt relief. Such coincidences might reflect the way that debt encourages loss of autonomy or dependency.

Potential investment has already influenced political relationships. El Salvador, for instance, cut ties with Taiwan in summer 2018 and switched allegiances to China, after Taiwanese engineers had reportedly declared a port project that the country sought loans for economically unfeasible[465]. The Dominican Republic also aligned with China at the expense of Taiwan in May 2018, following offers of US$3.1 billion in investment from China[466]. Likewise, Panama and Sao Tome e Principe cut diplomatic ties with Taiwan in 2017 and 2016 respectively before seeking investment from Beijing. In this way the expansion of Chinese capital overseas further impacts on global politics.

Geo-political Impacts

China has long stated a position of non-interference in the internal affairs of other countries, dating back to the Five Principals of Peaceful Coexistence for relations between states (including mutual respect for territorial integrity and sovereignty, mutual non-aggression, mutual non-interference in each other's internal affairs, equality and cooperation for mutual benefit and peaceful co-existence) that were first codified in 1954 in an agreement between China and India and later incorporated into the Bandung declaration. This policy, combined with the legacy of hardship inflicted as a result of loans and debt associated with Western lending and structural adjustment programs on which loans have sometimes been conditioned, has sometimes made Chinese investment and loans more attractive to developing countries than those from the West. Indeed, continued emphasis on its policy of non-interference allows China, at least on the surface, to present itself and its investments as different, even if many of the associated impacts concerning labour rights violations and environmental abuses may bear similarities from earlier and existing lenders and investments from other countries. Moreover, for China, while this position has an additional advantage in allowing it to continue to justify economic relations with countries in the face of other repressive regimes and human rights violations, the meaning of non-interference might be questioned when, in order to receive Chinese loans and investment, governments are required or put under pressure to overlook or bend local laws and regulations for the benefit of Chinese investors and turn a blind eye to the environmental and social consequences. When investment results in impacts on territorial integrity and the ceding of land and resources, this too necessarily shapes parts of a country's self-determination. Furthermore, that some countries have switched political allegiances coinciding with promises of investment might also be considered indirect interference.

The BRI has also heightened rivalries and tensions with existing economic powers.

A notable example from Asia is the China-India rivalry. From the beginning, China expected that India would take part in the BRI initiative as former prime minister Manmohan Singh's government had previously expressed support for the initiative. However new prime minister Narendra Modi's government has been opposed to it. India has concerns over the harm BRI will do to its own geostrategic interests and how it may detrimentally impact on India's influence in the region[467]. India has subsequently not officially participated in the BRI. According to some analysts, heightened tensions and confrontations along the Line of Control between India and China, which have seen violent face-offs and loss of life, are a sign of Beijing wanting to assert its dominance in the region and punish India for rejecting the BRI[468]. As noted earlier, alongside the aim of securing important communications and trade channels, wanting to assert its dominance in the region is likely a key reason for China's increasingly high-profile stance in the South China Sea as well.

While China may have increasingly begun to flex its muscles militarily, it has been keen to portray its global economic rise as a peaceful one and its overseas economic initiative, at least as far as financing is concerned, not as one of competition but of collaboration. Nevertheless, the expansion of China's economic significance, including its overseas investments, and the growing influence of China's corporations have been alarming to some countries and seen other (albeit smaller) investment initiatives initiated by rival countries likely intended at least in part to mitigate China's growing influence. In addition to this, in some developed countries in particular, concerns over perceived security risks, for instance related to Huawei technology, have seen a cooling in attitudes towards Chinese investments to some degree. The issue of trade deficits with China[469] have also been another sore point, with the US trade deficit with Chinaparticularly politically sensitive, sparking the US-China trade war which has had negative consequences for employment in both countries[470].

Looking forward: Covid-19 and the limits of Chinese overseas investments

The coronavirus pandemic has caused disruption to manufacturing supply chains and to the movement of persons, impacting on some BRI projects which rely on Chinese materials and labour. When the virus broke out globally, Beijing repatriated citizens working in some countries, for instance Iran, and by the end of April 2020 more than 130 countries placed entry restrictions on Chinese citizens or those traveling from China[471]. In June, the Chinese Foreign Ministry announced that 20% of BRI projects had been affected by the Covid-19 pandemic, while a survey by the Foreign Ministry estimated that 30-40% of projects had been somewhat affected and only 40% of projects had seen little adverse impact[472]. Given China's lack of transparency and history of exaggerating or manipulating statistics to paint an overly positive picture, it is not unreasonable to believe that this is an underestimation. With the future and long-term impact of the virus still very uncertain, it is difficult to fully assess how this may continue to shape the BRI. Will the pandemic further reduce the capacity for the number or BRI projects to grow or be fulfilled, or will China be able to re-strategise and prioritise other sectors such as health or digital industries? Even if a full recovery is made such that the pandemic ceases to be an obstacle, BRI projects and the expansion of Chinese investments overseas still face significant challenges and by no means offer a smooth path for China. While political and economic rivalries (for instance the US-China trade war) are also major factors, and despite more and more countries have been signing up to the BRI, increasing criticism has emerged along with the adverse impacts of BRI projects. This has sometimes contributed to the disruption delay, or cancellations of some projects.

Many of the problems linked to Chinese projects and investments, such as environmental destruction, labour rights violations, corruption and other malpractices are not unique to Chinese capital. However, Chinese capital and its investment overseas is significant for a number of reasons. This is not least because of the speed at which China has transformed itself and come to play such an important role in the global economy, rising to become a leading exporter of capital at such a rapid rate. The degree to which the expansion of China's overseas investments patterns is guided, controlled, and given significant political weight by the party-state is also notable. This is something which is not only a distinctive feature of Chinese overseas investments in their own right but is also significant due to the way that the Chinese state has come to be viewed as a rival to the influence of existing powers. While in many cases China has actually worked alongside, rather than as a competitor to, existing institutions such as the IMF, Chinese loans and investment have been presented as an alternative option to exploitation and investment by western countries and the legacy of colonialism (a view that China has encouraged). Nevertheless, this report has illustrated that, despite what China may claim, Chinese overseas investments do not offer desirable alternatives to investments from other powerful nations. Although Chinese capital does have its own characteristics, as another form of capital that has come to have devastating impacts on human and environmental health, it should also be challenged where it threatens to impact adversely on local people and the environment.

Strategies and Recommendations

In view of some of the problems arising from Chinese overseas investment and the challenges posed to people and the environment, what might civil society organisations and affected interest groups do to counteract, improve or limit adverse effects of the investment? And what might be done to help defend the rights and interests of workers and local populations in recipient countries?

China is a powerful actor and the BRI and associated Chinese overseas investments represent part of its current political and economic vision for the global arena. Challenging this vision is no easy task. But this does not mean that improvements to different situations on a case-by-case basis cannot be made in the interests of workers, local people and the environment that may add up to encourage better practices. While each country is different and strategies and tactics will need to be adapted to local situations, cross-border sharing of information and experiences allow us to gain greater knowledge of this powerful actor and its investments, which in turn might be used to inform and take action more effectively both in individual and collective cases and countries.

Below is a list of suggested starting points and questions to consider. These suggestions are not solutions in their own right but starting points, identifying potential areas around which to apply pressure to advocate for change and improvements. The list is not exhaustive either. Rather it is simply hoped that it may be of some use to initiating further exploration and discussion with a view to actions being taken on the ground.

Prior to agreement/ investment/commencement of a project

- Host countries of Chinese investment should insist on terms ensuring protecting good labour conditions for all workers and the provision of skills training for local workers as part of investment agreements and project tenders. Can local civil society lobby governments in host countries to ensure this?

- Will the project create well paid decent jobs locally? Where workers will be hired from China, can steps be taken to ensure that this is carried out in accordance with local laws and regulation, and can these workers be provided with information to help them integrate with local communities and to provide them with knowledge of their legal rights and how to protect them?

- Will the project have a positive impact on local communities and society?

- Will the project harm the environment? Have meaningful and valid Environmental Impact Assessments been carried out and are steps being taken to protect the environment? If the project will cause potential harm, is it possible to ensure widespread awareness of this and build a campaign against the project?

- Lending institutions: which organisations will be financing the project? What are their environmental and social impact criteria? Is it possible to put pressure on lending institutions to increase minimum standards of social responsibility?

- Is it possible to reach out to other communities affected by similar investment and learn from their experiences?

- Can relevant laws, regulations and grievance mechanisms governing the project be mapped out?

Post commencement of a project

- Legal Redress: Have there been violations of local laws? What are the mechanisms to hold companies accountable?

- Supply Chains: How do the Chinese companies (especially in manufacturing) fit into global supply chains? Can buyer and consumer pressure have an impact on overseas activities, especially as Chinese brands become more well-known?

- Lending institutions: is the project meeting their social and environmental commitments? Are they aware of any violations or malpractices?

- Worker organising: are there trade unions or community organisations that might be able to support workers? Are the affected workers already members of a trade union? If so, how supportive is it being? Is it possible to contact/support / build links between local and imported Chinese workers?

- International solidarity: While the problem of a lack of freedom of association and a genuine union in China makes solidarity between workers' organisations in mainland China and recipient countries more challenging, can international solidarity and worker exchanges be built between workers in different overseas countries affected by Chinese investment (and could this include workers in HK)?

Upon completion of a project

- Is the investment useful and is it having a positive impact on local communities? Is any infrastructure constructed being used?

- Are there any negative impacts on local communities and the environment?

- Are there mechanisms to report or put a halt to any damage being done?

- Have those promised compensation received it in full and are they satisfied with the situation? If not can further support be provided to remedy any problems?

- Might experiences with this investment or project be useful to other groups facing similar projects in mitigating any adverse impacts? Is it possible to make this information available?

REFERENCES

1 Remarks on India and the United States: A Vision for the 21st Century. Hillary Rodham Clinton. July 20, 2011. Chennai, India. https://2009-2017.state.gov/secretary/20092013clinton/rm/2011/07/168840.htm [Accessed 11th March 2020].

2 In December 2019, a GDP growth rate of 6% was reported, representing a record low for the period.

3 Au, LY. And Li K. (2011). Preliminary Report on China's Going Global Strategy: A Labour Environment and Hong Kong Perspective. Globalization Monitor.

4 It should be noted that this figure excludes companies from Taiwan but does include companies from Hong Kong.

5 Zheng, YP. In a first, China has more companies on Fortune Global 500 List than the US. 22md July 2019. South China Morning Post. https://www.scmp.com/business/companies/article/3019632/first-china-has-more-companies-fortune-global-500-list-us [Accessed 3rd November 2020].

6 Frankopan, P. (2019). The New Silk Roads: The Present and Future of the World. London: Bloomsbury.

7 Vision and Actions on Jointly Building Silk Road Economic Belt and 21st Century Maritime Silk Road. National Development and Reform Commission, Ministry of Foreign Affairs and Ministry of Commerce of the People's Republic of China. March 2015.

8 The Economist Intelligence Unit. (2017). China Going Global Investment Index 2017. www.eiu.com

9 MOFCOM Department of Outward Investment and Economic Coopera>on Comments on China's Outward Investment and Coopera>on in 2018. Ministry of Commerce. 17th January 2018.
h^p://english.mofcom.gov.cn/ar>cle/newsrelease/policyreleasing/201901/20190102829745.shtml
[Accessed 3rd November 2020].

10 Vision and Actions on Jointly Building Silk Road Economic Belt and 21st Century Maritime Silk Road. NDRC.

11 Frankopan, P. (2019). The New Silk Roads.

12 Au, LY. And Li K. (2011). Preliminary Report on China's Going Global Strategy.

13 Payne, J. Chinese commodity backed loans crippling Africa and Latin America. 26th February 2020. Reuters. Available from: https://www.reuters.com/article/commodities-loans-africa-americas/chinese-commodity-backed-loans-crippling-africa-and-latin-america-report-idUSL5N2AP3NL [Accessed 3rd November 2020]..

14 Miller, T. (2017). China's Asian Dream: Empire Building Along the New Silk Road. London: Zed Books.

15 Overcapacity in China. An Impediment to the Party's Reform Agenda. European Chamber of Commerce in China. 2016.

16 Sun, N. (2018). China Development Bank commits $250bn to Belt and Road. Nikkei Asian Review. https://asia.nikkei.com/Politics-Economy/Economy/China-Development-Bank-commits-250bn-to-Belt-and-Road [Accessed 11. Dec. 2018].

17 Miller, T. (2017). China's Asian Dream.

18 Lee, R. (2017). An introduction to the China-Pakistan Economic Corridor. Borderless Movement. https://borderless-hk.com/2017/08/16/an-introduction-to-the-china-pakistan-economic-corridor/ [Accessed 11. Dec. 2018].

19 Shattuck, T.J. (2020). The Race to Zero?: China's Poaching of Taiwan's Diplomatic Allies. Orbis 64 (2).

20 Au, LY. And Li K. (2011). Preliminary Report on China's Going Global Strategy.

21 https://www.ft.com/content/28f6b8d4-59cd-11e4-9787-00144feab7de

22 China ODI surpassed FDI for the first time in 2015. 29th September 2016. KPMG. https://home.kpmg/cn/en/home/insights/2016/09/china-odi-exceeded-fdi-2015-private-sector.html [Accessed 3rd November 2020].

23 FDI in Figures. OECD. October 2019.

24 China's Outward Investment in 2018: 5 point summary. 20th January 2019. Belt & Road Advisory. https://beltandroad.ventures/beltandroadblog/china-2018-overseas-investment-odi [Accessed 3rd November 2020.

25 Au, LY. And Li K. (2011). Preliminary Report on China's Going Global Strategy.

26 Xinhua. China's private sector contributes greatly to economic growth: federation leader. 6th March 2018. Available from: http://www.xinhuanet.com/english/2018-03/06/c_137020127.htm [Accessed 3rd October 2020].

27 NDB. 国资委副主任徐福顺：推动央企开展"一带一路"高质量合作. 20th September 2018. Available from: http://www.nbd.com.cn/articles/2018-09-20/1256965.html [Accessed 3rd October 2020].

28 Frankopan, P. (2019). The New Silk Roads.

29 Xinhua. China signs more trade deals with Belt and Road countries. 31st May 2018.

30 In these cases, the company finances and constructs a project, operates it for a fixed time period and then transfers it over to the host country's government.

31 Leutert, W. The Overseas Expansion and Evolution of Chinese State-Owned Enterprises.11th July 2019. Fairbank Center Blog. Available from: https://medium.com/fairbank-center/the-overseas-expansion-and-evolution-of-chinese-state-owned-enterprises-3dc04134c5f2 [Accessed 3rd November 2020].

32 Defined as 'government aid designed to promote the economic development and welfare of developing countries' ... Aid includes grants, "soft" loans (where the grant element is at least 25% of the total) and the provision of technical assistance". OECD Data. Net ODA. Organisation for Economic Co-operation and Development. https://data.oecd.org/oda/net-oda.htm. [Accessed 11 Dec. 2018].

33 AidData. (2017). China's Global Development Footprint. https://www.aiddata.org/china-official-finance [Accessed 8. Dec.2018].

34 Grimsditch, M. The Role and Characteristics of Chinese State-owned and Private Enterprises in Overseas Investments. June 2015. Friends of the Earth.

35 Latham and Watkins. China Issues Formal Guidance for Outbound Direct Investments. Latham and Watkins. August 2017. https://www.lw.com/thoughtLeadership/LW-China-Issues-Formal-Guidance-for-Outbound-Direct-Investments

36 He, L. Having dumped US $25 billion in assets, Wanda still about halfway through cutting its debt burden. 10th April 2019. South China Morning Post. https://www.scmp.com/business/china-business/article/3005385/having-dumped-us25-billion-assets-wanda-still-about-halfway [Accessed 3rd November 2020]

37 Marks, S. China in Africa. 2007

38 Phoenix Weekly. Chinese overseas investment hindered by lack of experience, political opposition in host countries. 14th September 2015. https://www.globaltimes.cn/content/942349.shtml [Accessed 3rd November 2020].

39 Chu, Y. (2016). Loan rate for China-Thai railway reflects market conditions. Global Times. Available from: http://www.globaltimes.cn/content/979886.shtml [Accessed 18. Dec. 2018]

40 Barrow, K. China-Europe rail freight: in it for the long haul. International Railway Journal. 17th January 2018. Available from: https://www.railjournal.com/in_depth/china-europe-rail-freight-in-it-for-the-long-haul [Accessed 3rd November 2020]

41 Babones, S. The New Eurasian Land Bridge Linking China and Europe Makes No Economic Sense, So Why Build It? Forbes. 28th December 2017. https://www.forbes.com/sites/salvatorebabones/2017/12/28/the-new-eurasian-land-bridge-linking-china-and-europe-makes-no-economic-sense-so-why-build-it/#1e3b420a5c9c [Accessed 3rd November 2020].

42 Barrow, K. China-Europe rail freight.

43 Xinhua. Construction begins in China-Mongolia cross-border economic zone. Xinhua. 21st September 2017. http://www.xinhuanet.com//english/2017-09/21/c_136626788.htm [Accessed 3rd November 2020]

44 Xinhua. China Focus: China-Mongolia trade in steady progress. Xinhua. 11th July 2019. http://www.xinhuanet.com/english/2019-07/11/c_138218105.htm [Accessed 3rd November 2020]

45 Shah, A. China, Russia and the Case of the Missing Bridge. The Diplomat. 20th November 2018. https://thediplomat.com/2018/11/china-russia-and-the-case-of-the-missing-bridge/ [Accessed 3rd November 2020].

46 Stolyarov, G. Russia and China deepen ties with River Amur bridge. Reuters. 29th November 2019. https://www.reuters.com/article/russia-china-bridge/russia-and-china-deepen-ties-with-river-amur-bridge-idUSL8N28920Y [Accessed 3rd November 2020]

47 Ministry of Foreign Affairs. Li Keqiang Meets with President Khaltmaa Battulga of Mongolia. 24th April 2019. https://www.fmprc.gov.cn/mfa_eng/zxxx_662805/t1658173.shtml [Accessed 3rd November 2020]

48 Judge, C. What does the China-Russia-Mongolia Economic Corridor mean for Mongolia? Belt & Road Advisory. 30th September 2018. https://beltandroad.ventures/beltandroadblog/china-mongolia-russia-economic-corridor [Accessed 3rd November 2020].

49 China-Central Asia -West Asia Economic Corridor. 9th April 2017. http://www.china.org.cn/english/china_key_words/2017-04/19/content_40651859.htm [Accessed 4th November 2020]

50 Yellinek, R. The Impact of China's Belt and Road Initiative on Central Asia and the South Caucuses. 26th February 2020. E-International Relations. Available at https://isnblog.ethz.ch/trade/the-impact-of-chinas-belt-and-road-initiative-on-central-asia-and-the-south-caucasus [Accessed 4th November 2020]

51 Lai, YW and Wu, A. China-Central Asia-Western Economic Corridor: Progress, Main Challenges and Promotion Measures (No.187, 2018) Development Research Centre of the State Council of the People's Republic of China. http://en.drc.gov.cn/2019-01/02/content_37421873.htm [Accessed 4th November 2020]

52 HKTDC. The ASEAN Link in China's Belt and Road Initiative. 30th September 2015. HKTDC Research. http://hkmb.hktdc.com/en/1X0A3UUO/hktdc-research/The-ASEAN-Link-in-China%E2%80%99s-Belt-and-Road-Initiative [Accessed 4th November 2020]

53 Chin, S. Trans-Asian Railway chugs closer to becoming a reality. 14th July 2018. Asean Post. https://theaseanpost.com/article/trans-asian-railway-chugs-closer-becoming-reality [Accessed 4th November 2020]

54 Lewis, S. and Vannarin, N. Report Shows Lack of Information on Chinese Funded Railway. 7th March 2013. The Cambodian Daily. https://english.cambodiadaily.com/news/report-shows-lack-of-information-on-chinese-funded-railway-12723/ [Accessed 4th November 2020]

55 Nanning-Chingzuo Intercity Railway to open by 20201. 14th February 2019. China Daily. http://govt.chinadaily.com.cn/a/201902/14/WS5c6b59b8498e27e3380388ab.html [Accessed 4th November 2020]

56 Lee, R. An introduction to the China-Pakistan Economic Corridor. 11th June 2020. https://www.globalmon.org.hk/node/1701 [Accessed 4th November 2020]

57 China drops BCIM from BRI projects' list. 28th April 2019. Business Standard. https://www.business-standard.com/article/news-ians/china-drops-bcim-from-bri-projects-list-119042800540_1.html [Accessed 4th November 2020]

58 Chuadhury, D. R. Kunming meet revives BCIM plan. 24th June 2019. The Economic Times. https://economictimes.indiatimes.com/news/politics-and-nation/kunming-meet-revives-bcim-link-plan/articleshow/69921135.cms [Accessed 4th November 2020]

59 Peter, K. China and the 21st Century Maritime Silk Road. 16th March 2017. PAGEO Research Institute http://www.geopolitika.hu/en/2017/03/16/china-and-the-21st-century-new-maritime-silk-road/ [Accessed 4th November 2020]

60 China's Arctic Policy. The State Council Information Office of the People's Republic of China. January 2018. First Edition. https://eng.yidaiyilu.gov.cn/zchj/qwfb/46076.htm [Accessed 4th November 2020]

61 In 2018 China established a new agency, the State International Development Cooperation Agency (SIDCA). The agency is responsible to the State Council and responsible for formulating guidelines and policies on foreign aid. Its most recent work seems largely to have involved donating medical supplies to fight Covid-19 to various countries around the world.

62 Defined as 'government aid designed to promote the economic development and welfare of developing countries' … Aid includes grants, "soft" loans (where the grant element is at least 25% of the total) and the provision of technical assistance". See: (OECD Data)

63 By way of comparison, US aid for the same period was $424bn and was almost all concessional and/or in the form of grants

64 A new study tracks the surge in Chinese loans to poor countries. 13th July 2018. The Economist. https://www.economist.com/finance-and-economics/2019/07/13/a-new-study-tracks-the-surge-in-chinese-loans-to-poor-countries [Accessed 4th November 2020]

65 AidData. (2017). China's Global Development Footprint. [online]. https://www.aiddata.org/china-official-finance [Accessed 8. Dec.2018].
66 A new study tracks the surge in Chinese loans to poor countries. 13th July 2018. The Economist.

67 Peng, Q and Jia, D. (2017). China State Banks Provide over $400 Bln of Credits to Belt and Road Projects. Caixin. [online]. https://www.caixinglobal.com/2017-05-12/101089361.html [Accessed 11. Dec. 2018].

68 China Development Bank 2018 Annual Report.

69 Provaggi, A. China Devlopment Bank's financing mechanisms: focus on foreign investment. Global Projects Center.

70 China Development Bank. About CDB. http://www.cdb.com.cn/English/gykh_512/khjj/ [Accessed 4th November 2020].

71 China Development Bank 2018 Annual Report.

72 Ibid

73 Chinese lending and the Venezuelan Crisis. 13th March 2018. Globalization Monitor. https://www.globalmon.org.hk/content/chinese-lending-and-venezuelan-crisis [Accessed 4th November 2020]

74 Zhang, S. and Miller, M. Behind China's Silk Road vision: cheap funds, heavy debt, growing risk. 15th May 2017. Reuters. https://www.reuters.com/article/us-china-silkroad-finance/behind-chinas-silk-road-vision-cheap-funds-heavy-debt-growing-risk-idUSKCN18B0YS [Accessed 4th November 2020]

75 Sun, N. (2018). China Development Bank commits $250bn to Belt and Road. Nikkei Asian Review. https://asia.nikkei.com/Politics-Economy/Economy/China-Development-Bank-commits-250bn-to-Belt-and-Road [Accessed 11. Dec. 2018]

76 Zhang, YZ., Ji, TQ and Lin, JB. Prosecutors Sign Off on Arrest of Former Boss of Policy Bank CDB. 13th February 2020. Caixin. https://www.caixinglobal.com/2020-02-13/prosecutors-sign-off-on-arrest-of-former-boss-of-policy-bank-cdb-101515070.html [Accessed 4th November 2020]

77 The Export-Import Bank of China Annual Report 2018.

78 Ibid

79 Zhang, S. and Miller, M. Behind China's Silk Road vision

80 Peng, Q and Jia, D. (2017).

81 Wright, C. Making Sense of Belt and Road — The Chinese Commercial Bank ICBC. 26th September 2017. Euro Money https://www.euromoney.com/article/b14t12brg3ynxd/making-sense-of-belt-and-road-the-chinese-commercial-bank-icbc [Accessed 4th November 2020]

82 Chen, C. Can ICBC Asia profit from China's new Silk Road projects? 25th June 2017. South China Morning Post. https://www.scmp.com/business/banking-finance/article/2099907/can-icbc-asia-profit-chinas-new-silk-road-projects [Accessed 4th November 2020]

83 Xi Jinping has since pledged an additional 100 million RMB for the fund.

84 Silk Road Fund. Overview. http://www.silkroadfund.com.cn/enweb/23775/23767/index.html [Accessed 4th November 2020]

85 China's CITIC to invest $113 billion for Silk Road investments. 24th June 2015. Reuters. https://www.reuters.com/article/china-citic-investments-idUSL3N0ZA3AH20150624 [Accessed 4th November 2020]
86 Shang, HP. The Belt and Road Initiative: Key Concepts. 2019. pp99-100

87 HSBC. Belt and Road award for HSBC. 25th September

2019. HSBC. https://www.hsbc.com/who-we-are/hsbc-news/belt-and-road-award-for-hsbc [Accessed 4th November 2020]

88 Morangi, L. Banks see opportunities in Belt and Road Initiative.19th April 2019. China Daily. http://www.chinadailyglobal.com/a/201904/19/WS5cb91a49a3104842260b70d9.html [Accessed 4th November 2020]

89 Wei, YY., and Liu, JF. China-Led Development Bank Chief Says More Lending on Way After Slow Start. Caixin. 9th November 2018. https://www.caixinglobal.com/2018-11-09/china-led- development-bank-chief-says-more-lending-on-way-after-slow-start-101345233.html [Accessed 4th November 2020]

90 Babones, S. (2018). China's AIIB Expected to Lend $10-15B A Year, But Has Only Managed S4.4B .n Two Years. Forbes. https://www.forbes.com/sites/salvatorebabones/2018/01/16/chinas-aiib-expected-to-lend-10-15b-a-year-but-has-only-managed-4-4b-in-2-years/#36a3bafd37f1 [Accessed 11. Dec. 2018].

91 Ayres, M. BRICS nations to study adding countries to development bank. 12th November 2019. Reuters. Available from: https://www.reuters.com/article/us-brics-summit-bank/brics-nations-to-study-adding-countries-to-development-bank-idUSKBN1XM2KK [Accessed 4th November 2020]

92 New Development Bank. (2018). Procurement Policy. Version 2018 V1.

93 CBRC. Green Credit Guidelines. 2012. China Banking Regulatory Commission. http://www.cbrc.gov.cn/EngdocView.do?docID=3CE646AB629B46B9B533B1D8D9FF8C4A

94 Bohoslavsky, J. P. A Human Rights Focus to Upgrade China's International Lending. The Chinese Journal of Global Governance 5 (1). March 2019.

95 Ibid

96 Au, LY. And Li K. (2011). Preliminary Report on China's Going Global Strategy: A Labour Environment and Hong Kong Perspective. Globalization Monitor.
97 Ibid

98 Ibid

99 Outward Foreign Direct Investment: A Novel Dimension of China's Integration into the Regional and Global Economy. Kevin Cai. 1999. The China Quarterly. 160 pp.856-880

100 Xia, L. China's numbers don't tell full story on foreign investment. 23rd June 2015. https://asia.nikkei.com/Economy/China-s-numbers-don-t-tell-full-story-on-foreign-investment [Accessed 16th November 2020] Xiao, G. People's Republic of China's Round-Tripping FDI: Scale, Causes and Implications. July 2004. ADB Institute Discussion Paper No. 7.

101 Ibid.

102 Yim, S. Economic and Trade Information on Hong Kong. 13th November 2020. HKTDC Research. https://research.hktdc.com/en/article/MzIwNjkzNTY5 [Accessed 16th November 2020]

103 Vision and Actions on Jointly Building Silk Road Economic Belt and 21st Century Maritime Silk Road.National Development and Reform Commission, Ministry of Foreign Affairs and Ministry of Commerce of the People's Republic of China. March 2015.

104 Yau, E. Belt-Road Connects People's Nations. Belt-Road connects people, nations. 11th September 2017. http://www.news.gov.hk/en/record/html/2017/09/20170911_173308.shtml?pickList=ticker [Accessed 16th November 2020]

105 Ibid

106 The concept of the Greater Bay Area had been mentioned several years prior to this.

107 External Direct Investment Statistics of Hong Kong 2018. December 2019. Census and Statistics Department: Hong Kong Special Administrative Region
108 Ibid

109 Ibid

110 Yim, S. Economic and Trade Information on Hong Kong.

111 Yiu, E. and He, L. Hong Kong has played an outsized role in contributing to the growth of China's financial market. 3rd December 2018. South China Morning Post. https://www.scmp.com/business/article/2175980/hong-kong-has-played-outsize-role-contributing-growth-chinas-financial [Accessed 16th November 2020]
112 Yim, S. Economic and Trade Information on Hong Kong.

113 Huang, TL. Why China still needs Hong Kong. 15th July 2019. Peterson Institute for International Economics. https://www.piie.com/blogs/china-economic-watch/why-china-still-needs-hong-kong#_ftn2 [Accessed 16th November 2020] and Market Statistics 2018. HKEX.
114 Outward Foreign Direct Investment: A Novel Dimension of China's Integration into the Regional and Global Economy. Kevin Cai. 1999. The China Quarterly. 160 pp. 856-880.

115 Yiu, E. Belt and Road set to rekindle interest in Hong Kong's red chips. 12th August 2016. South China Morning Post: http://www.scmp.com/business/companies/article/2002975/belt-and-road-set-rekindle-interest-hong-kongs-red-chips [Accessed 16th November 2020]

116 Ibid

117 Ibid

118 HKEX currently has two boards — the main board and the Growth Enterprise Market (GEM). To list on the main board companies are required to have made a combined profit of HK$50 million in the three years prior to their listing. Admission requirements for the GEM are less stringent and this board acts as a steppingstone to the main board. There are plans for a third board to be created exclusively for new technology companies

119 Market Statistic 2019. HKEX

120 Hong Kong's Role in Supporting the Fund-Raising of Mainland Private Enterprises. June 2019. HKEX Research Papers.

121 Ibid

122 Making Inroads: Chinese Infrastructure Investment in ASEAN and Beyond. 2016. Inclusive Development International.

123 This in itself is nothing new, as development plans promoting greater integration between Hong Kong and Guangdong have often been presented that have come to very little in the past.

124 Chung, K. Former Hong Kong leader CY Leung denies conflict of interest over 'Belt and Road' company directorship. 12th September 2017. South China Morning Post.http://www.scmp.com/news/hong-kong/politics/article/2110883/former-hong-kong-leader-cy-leung-denies-conflict-interest [Accessed 16th November 2020]

125 Su, XQ. And Siu, P. Hong Kong-Zhuhai-Macau mega bridge project set to exceed budget by more than HK$11 billion. 21st November 2017. South China Morning Post. https://www.scmp.com/news/hong-kong/economy/article/2120965/hong-kong-zhuhai-macau-mega-bridge-project-set-exceed-budget [Accessed 16th November 2020]

126 Vines, S. How much is life worth? Not much, if measured by fines for employer negligence in Macau bridge construction. 30th August 2020. Hong Kong Free Press. https://hongkongfp.com/2020/08/30/how-much-is-a-life-worth-not-much-if-measured-by-fines-for-employer-negligence-in-macau-bridge-construction/ [Accessed 16th November 2020]

127 Chan, L. Experts blame Hong Kong-Zhuhai-Macau Bridge for falling dolphin numbers. 16th July 2016. South China Morning Post. https://www.scmp.com/news/hong-kong/health-environment/article/1990312/experts-blame-hong-kong-zhuhai-macau-bridge [Accessed 16th November 2020]

128 Belt and Road Summit Side Trip: Guangdong-Hong Kong-Macao Bay Area (Zhuhai and Zhongshan) http://www.beltandroadsummit.hk/en/information_centre/side_trip.html Accessed 6th Sept. 2017

129 Su, XQ. Hong Kong's bridge to Zhuhai to allow 7,000 extra cars to cross after 'overwhelming demand for permits. 12th December 2017. South China Morning Post. https://www.scmp.com/news/hong-kong/economy/article/2124010/hong-kongs-bridge-zhuhai-allow-7000-extra-cars-cross-after [Accessed 16th November 2020]

130 Ho, P. Chinese giants are taking over Hong Kong. 7th June 2017. Bloomberg. https://www.bloomberg.com/news/features/2017-06-06/chinese-giants-are-taking-over-hong-kong [Accessed 16th November 2020]

131 Zheng, YP. Hong Kong receives 80 per cent of China's outbound property investment in second quarter. 2nd August 2018. South China Morning Post. https://www.scmp.com/business/money/markets-investing/article/2157909/hong-kong-receives-80pc-chinas-outbound-property [Accessed 16th November 2020]

132 Nguy, D. Lui fears local players edged out. 25th November 2016. The Standard https://www.thestandard.com.hk/section-news/section/2/176759/Lui-fears-local-players-edged-out [Accessed 15th November 2020]

133 Yam, S. Beijing wants tycoons to take action, not just pay lip service. 1st November 2014. South China Morning Post. http://www.scmp.com/business/article/1629442/beijing-wants-tycoons-take-action-not-just-pay-lip-service?page=all [Accessed 15th November 2020]

134 COSCO Shipping. Group Profile. http://en.coscoshipping.com/col/col6918/index.html [Accessed 15th April 2020]

135 SASAC. What we do. http://en.sasac.gov.cn/2018/07/17/c_7.htm. [Accessed 12th June 2019]

136 Wang, Y. COSCO Shipping rides the BRI wave. 14th May 2019. China Daily. https://www.chinadaily.com.cn/a/201905/14/WS5cda25d7a3104842260bb7e6.html [Accessed 10th November 2020]

137 Pamuk, H. and Gardner, T. U.S. lifts Iran sanctions on one unit Chinese shipping giant COSCO. 30th January 2020. Reuters. https://www.reuters.com/article/us-iran-nuclear-usa-cosco/u-s-lifts-iran-sanctions-on-one-unit-of-chinese-shipping-giant-cosco-idUSKBN1ZU04I [Accessed 10th November 2020]

138 Ibid

139 COSCO SHIPPING Ports Ltd. About CSP: Corporate Profile. https://ports.coscoshipping.com/en/AboutCSP/CorporateProfile/Overview/ [Accessed 10th November 2020]

140 Swift, R. Cosco Shipping's rising container volumes put it on course to overtake Hutchison Ports as world's no.2 port operator. 1st September 2019. South China Morning Post. https://www.scmp.com/business/companies/article/3025127/cosco-shippings-rising-container-volumes-put-it-course-overtake [Accessed 10th November 2020]

141 Shareholding percentages are based on those provided in the company's 2019 Annual Report.

142 Van der Putten, FP. Chinese Investment in the Port of Pireaus, Greece: The Relevance for the EU and the Netherlands. 14th February 2014. Clingendael Report. Netherlands Institute of International Relations.

143 COSCO Shipping. About Us. http://www.coscointl.com/en/about-us/cosco-shipping-hong-kong/overview/ [Accessed 10th November 2020]

144 Xinhua. Xi, Greek PM visit Pireaus Port, hail BRI cooperation. 12th November 2019. Available at http://www.xinhuanet.com/english/2019-11/12/c_138548572.htm [Accessed 10th November 2020]

145 COSCO Shipping Ports Limited. Annual Report 2019.

146 Cited in: COSCO urges multilateral benefits in overseas business. Ren Xiaojin. 8th April 2019 China Daily. https://www.chinadaily.com.cn/a/201904/08/WS5caaf5fea3104842260b4f07.html [Accessed 15th November 2020]

147 COSCO Shipping. COSCO Shipping Acquired a 60% Stake in a Greek Railway Company. 15th November 2019. http://en.coscoshipping.com/art/2019/11/15/art_6923_124985.html [Accessed 10th November 2020]

148 China and Greece agree on $660m expansion of Piraeus Port. 12th November 2019. NIKKEI Asia. https://asia.nikkei.com/Politics/International-relations/China-and-Greece-agree-on-660m-expansion-of-Piraeus-Port [Accessed 10th November 2020]

149 This refers to the Third Economic Adjustment Programme agreed by Greece with the European Commission, IMF and European Central Bank in July 2015. In exchange for a financial bail-out, Greece had to agree to harsh austerity conditions and privatization of state assets. The port was fully sold-off to COSCO in this context in 2016.

150 CCCC. Introduction. China Communications Construction Company Ltd. http://en.ccccltd.cn/aboutcompany/introduction/. [Accessed 20th January 2019]

151 Ibid.

152 Alon, Ilan. A Guide to the Top 100 Companies in China. World Scientific.

153 CCCC. Introduction.

154 Shanghai Stock Exchange. 公司概况 http://www.sse.com.cn/assortment/stock/list/info/company/index.shtml?COMPANY_CODE=601800.[Accessed 20th January 2019]

155 HKEX. China Communications Construction Company Ltd — H Shares (1800). Available at https://www.hkex.com.hk/Market-Data/Securities-Prices/Equities/Equities-Quote?sym=1800&sc_lang=en. [Accessed 20th January 2019]

156 CCCC. 2018 3 Q Report. China Communications Construction Company Ltd.

157 Prasso, S. A Chinese Company Reshaping the World Leaves a Troubled Trail. 18th September 2018. https://www.bloomberg.com/news/features/2018-09-19/a-chinese-company-reshaping-the-world-leaves-a-troubled-trail [Accessed 10th November 2020]

158 Zhong, N. Construction giant CCCC aims to expand its global presence. 4th December 2018. China Daily. https://www.chinadaily.com.cn/a/201812/04/WS5c05e394a310eff30328ee34.html [Accessed 10th November 2020]

159 参考消息. 出海记｜1600多"一带一路"项目助中交建提升全球话语权, 24th April 2018. http://www.cankaoxiaoxi.com/finance/20180424/2263022.shtml. [Accessed 10th November 2020]

160 The World Bank. World Bank Applies 2009 Debarment to China Communications Construction Company Limited for Fraud in Philippines Roads Project. 29th July 2011. https://www.worldbank.org/en/news/press-release/2011/07/29/world-bank-applies-2009-debarment-to-china-communications-construction-company-limited-for-fraud-in-philippines-roads-project [Accessed 10th November 2020]

161 Prasso, S. A Chinese Company Reshaping the World Leaves a Troubled Trail.

162 Anonymous. Malaysia's East Coast Rail Link to cost US$20b, up 50% from estimates: Finance minister. 3rd July 2018. Channel News Asia, July 3, 2018.

163 郑世波. 通讯：泗马大桥见证中印尼友好关系发展，新华社. Xinhua. May 7, 2018.

164 Anonymous. 马来西亚槟城第二跨海大桥（槟城二桥）正式通车, 人民网, 1st March 2014. http://world.people.com.cn/n/2014/0301/c1002-24501687.html. [Accessed 10th November 2020]

165 Anonymous. 【总稽查司报告】收入不足还债 槟二桥连亏3年, 诗华日报, 7th August 2018. http://news.seehua.com/?p=382716. [Accessed 10th November 2020]

166 Second Engineering Company of CCCC Fourth Harbor Engineering Co., Ltd. http://www.fhebsc.com/show_ditail.php?curprog=3&id=679. [Accessed 20th January 2019]

167 Spotlight: Fourth Panama Canal Bridge shrouded in uncertainty. 30th August 2019. Bnamericas. https://www.bnamericas.com/en/news/spotlight-fourth-panama-canal-bridge-shrouded-in- uncertainty [Accessed 10th November 2020]

168 Buchholz, K. The Biggest Oil and Gas Companies in the World. 10th January 2020. Statista. https://www.statista.com/chart/17930/the-biggest-oil-and-gas-companies-in-the-world/ [Accessed 10th November 2020]

169 Sinopec. Leadership. http://www.sinopecgroup.com/group/en/companyprofile/Leadership/. [Accessed 13th June 2019]

170 General Office of the State Council of the People's Republic of China. 国务院关于组建中国石油化工集团公司有关问题的批复, July 21, 1998. http://www.gov.cn/xxgk/pub/govpublic/mrlm/201011/t20101120_62923.html. [Accessed 13th June 2019]

171 天眼查. 中国石油化工集团有限公司. https://www.tianyancha.com/company/3223702242. [Accessed 13th June 2019]

172 Anonymous. 【改革开放40年·国企轨迹㉕】中国石化：因改革而发展 在改革中壮大, 中国石油化工集团公司, December 19, 2018. http://www.sasac.gov.cn/n4470048/n8456886/n9847297/n9906617/c10025731/content.html. [Accessed 13th June 2019]

173 Anonymous. 中石化炼化工程（集团）股份有限公司在京揭牌, 中国新闻网, September 3, 2012. http://www.chinanews.com/ny/2012/09-03/4153581.shtml. [Accessed 13th June 2019]

174 Anonymous. 中石化炼化工程在港正式挂牌上市, 中国能源网, May 23, 2013. https://www.china5e.com/news/news-339392-1.html. [Accessed 13th June 2019]

175 Ibid.

176 Anonymous. 继续竞标伊朗油田中石化"盯紧"中东能源，搜狐，February 3, 2004. http://business.sohu.com/2004/02/03/17/article218881704.shtml. [Accessed 13th June 2019]

177 Anonymous. 中石化在伊朗打出高产油气井，搜狐，January 8, 2004. http://news.sohu.com/2004/01/08/81/news218168157.shtml. [Accessed 13th June 2019]

178 Ibid.]

179 Anonymous. 中石油人士：伊拉克动乱对中国在伊油田影响，人民网，June 18, 2014. http://energy.people.com.cn/n/2014/0618/c71661-25167651.html. [Accessed 13th June 2019]

180 Anonymous. 【改革开放 40 年·国企轨迹㉕】中国石化：因改革而发展 在改革中壮大，中国石油化工集团公司，December 19, 2018. http://www.sasac.gov.cn/n4470048/n8456886/n9847297/n9906617/c10025731/content.html. [Accessed 13th June 2019]

181 Anonymous. Joint venture sets model for China-Russia cooperation in energy field, China Daily, July 3, 2017. http://www.chinadaily.com.cn/business/2017-07/03/content_29972242.htm. [Accessed 13th June 2019]

182 Its full name is Tiptop Energy (BVI) Corporation, which was established on September 30, 2009 and is registered in the British Virgin Islands. It is wholly owned by Tiptop HK. The latter is registered in Hong Kong and wholly owned by Sinopec International Petroleum Exploration and Production Limited. Both Tiptop BVI and Tiptop HK are mainly engaged in investment holding. (Source: http://finance.sina.com.cn/stock/t/20130325/010014935300.shtml) [Accessed 13th June 2019]

183 Anonymous. 中石化实现对里海资源完全控股，CGGT 走出去智库，August 27, 2015. http://www.cggthinktank.com/2015-08-27/100074377.html. [Accessed 13th June 2019]

184 何清. 中石化无奈超高价位收购哈萨克油田，21 世纪财经，August 21, 2015. https://m.21jingji.com/article/20150821/herald/485faf6c0cd45a0f6f905d661e1c233e.html. [Accessed 13th June 2019]

185 Anonymous. Colombia takes back an oilfield from OVL, The Economic Times, October 14, 2008. 75

186 Charlie Zhu. Sinopec to pay $1.5 billion for parent's oil, gas assets, Reuters, March 25, 2013. https://www.reuters.com/article/us-sinopec-acquisition/sinopec-to-pay-1-5-billion-for-parents-oil-gas-assets-idUSBRE92N0CN20130325. [Accessed 13th June 2019]

187 Mansarovar Energy. Sustainability Report 2017.

188 Anonymous. 中国石化斥 5.6 亿美元向母公司收购沙特炼化项目部分权益，Reuters, October 31, 2014. https://cn.reuters.com/article/sinopec-sa-idCNKBS0IK02U20141031. [Accessed 13th June 2019]

189 王波. 通讯：探访中沙经贸合作典范延布炼厂，新华网，July 9, 2018. http://www.xinhuanet.com/fortune/2018-07/09/c_129909852.htm. [Accessed 13th June 2019]

190 YASREF. Yasref Overview https://www.yasref.com/en-us/Pages/About.aspx. [Accessed 13th June 2019]

191 Sonya Dowsett, Chen Aizhu. China's Sinopec buys Repsol Brazil stake for $7.1 billion, Reuters, Octorber 1, 2010. https://www.reuters.com/article/us-repsol-sinopec/chinas-sinopec-buys-repsol-brazil-stake-for-7-1-billion-idUSTRE6900YZ20101001. [Accessed 13th June 2019]

192 The official website of Repsol. Repsol Worldwide. https://www.repsol.com/en/repsol-worldwide/the-americas/brazil/index.cshtml. Accessed in July 1, 2019. [Accessed 13th June 2019]

193 田春. 石化：安哥拉项目疑云，新浪财经，April, 19, 2010.

194 Anonymous. 左手安哥拉右手中石化 中基模式尾大不掉，新浪财经，October 17, 2011. http://finance.sina.com.cn/roll/20111017/164110635622.shtml. [Accessed 13th June 2019]

195 Anonymous. Sinopec Signs $1b Abadan Refinery Expansion Deal, Financial Tribune, December 29, 2017. https://financialtribune.com/articles/energy/78896/sinopec-signs-1b-abadan-refinery-expansion-deal. [Accessed 13th June 2019]

196 Anonymous. Sinopec Persists With Iran Refinery Upgrade, Argus Blog, September 20, 2018. https://www.argusmedia.com/en/news/1757722-sinopec-persists-with-iran-refinery-upgrade. [Accessed 13th June 2019]

197 Anonymous. 中石化炼化工程拿下 70 海外大单，国际业务再次发力，搜狐，January 3, 2018. http://www.sohu.com/a/214374098_188371. [Accessed 13th June 2019]

198 Ibid.

199 Anonymous. SINOPEC Engineering : KNPC awards SEG the largest refinery project in the Middle East, MarketScreener, August 2, 2015. https://www.marketscreener.com/SINOPEC-ENGINEERING-GROUP-13266918/news/SINOPEC-Engineering-KNPC-awards-SEG-the-largest-refinery-project-in-the-Middle-East-20793765/. [Accessed 13th June 2019]

200 Ibid.

201 Anonymous. 中石化与马来西亚石油签署 13 亿美元合约，新浪财经，September 1, 2014. http://finance.sina.com.cn/energy/corpnews/20140901/104720178107.shtml. [Accessed 13th June 2019]

202 Ibid.

203 Anonymous. 中石化收购美国西方石油公司阿根廷资产，Reuters, December 10, 2010. https://cn.reuters.com/article/idCNCHINA-3480120101210. [Accessed 13th June 2019]
204 Ibid.

205 Anonymous. 石油三巨头 400 亿美元投资委内瑞拉，中国能源网, December 3, 2010. https://www.china5e.com/news/news-144166-1.html. [Accessed 13th June 2019]

206 Anonymous. 中石化收购阿帕奇在埃及资产 1/3 权益交易交割，新浪财经, http://finance.sina.com.cn/chanjing/gsnews/20131115/141617336485.shtml?luicode=20000061&lfid=3644912807106699. [Accessed 13th June 2019]

207 Ibid.

208 Anonymous. 中石化集团完成收购葡萄牙石油公司 Galp 巴西资产, Reuters, March 30, 2012. https://cn.reuters.com/article/sinopec-ma-galp-brazil-jw-idCNCNE82T04720120330. [Accessed 13th June 2019]

vv

209 Ibid.

210 Anonymous. 中石化与道达尔就收购尼日利亚一油田区块权益达成协议，第一财经, November 20, 2012. https://www.yicai.com/news/2261458.html. [Accessed 13th June 2019]

211 Ibid.

212 Scott, Haggett. Sinopec pays $1.5 billion for Talisman North Sea Stake, Reuters, July 23, 2012. https://www.reuters.com/article/us-sinopec-talisman/sinopec-pays-1-5-billion-for-talisman-north- sea-stake-idUSBRE86M0IL20120723. [Accessed 13th June 2019]

213 Ibid.

214 林晨音，杨铮．中石化花费 72 亿美元收购瑞士阿达克斯石油公司，搜狐, June 25, 2009. http://news.sohu.com/20090625/n264756355.shtml. [Accessed 13th June 2019]

215 Ibid.

216 The Environmental Impact of China's Investment in Africa. David H Shinn. 2016. Cornell International Law Journal. Vol.49.

217 These activities were subsequently resumed after new EIAs were carried out.

218 This is something that was acknowledged by the China Council for International Cooperation on Environment and Development, which stated in 2012 that Chinese companies were 15-20 years behind their Western counterparts in this respect.

219 Ibid

220 Ibid

221 CNPC, another Chinese oil giant, has the largest share in the consortium (41%).

222 Mednick, S. South Sudan buries reports on oil pollution, birth defects. 13th February 2020. Associated Press. https://abcnews.go.com/International/wireStory/south-sudan-ignores-reports-oil-pollution-birth-defects-68955924 [Accessed 10th November 2020]

223 Ibid

224 Cryderman, K. Sinopec unit fined $1.5-million over deaths at Alberta oil sands project. 24th January 2013 https://www.theglobeandmail.com/report-on-business/industry-news/the-law-page/sinopec-unit-fined-15-million-over-deaths-at-alberta-oil-sands-project/article7823202/ [Accessed 10th November 2020]

225 Ibid

226 China uncovers abuse of power, nepotism at Sinopec. 7th February 2015. Reuters. https://www.reuters.com/article/china-corruption-sinopec/china-uncovers-power-abuses-nepotism-at-sinopec-idUSL4N0VH03L20150207 [Accessed 10th November 2020]

227 Sinopec investigated for US$100m Nigeria kickbacks, reports says. 31st August 2017. The Standard. https://www.thestandard.com.hk/breaking-news/section/1/95929/Sinopec-investigated-for-US$100m-Nigeria-kickbacks,-report-says [Accessed 10th November 2020]

228 Sinopec plans Nigeria, Gabon sale. 12th December 2017. https://oglinks.news/sinopec/news/plans-nigeria-gabon-sale [Accessed 10th November 2020]

229 Ibid

230 Obiorah, N. Who's afraid of China in Africa? Towards an African civil society perspective on China-Africa relations. In: African perspectives in China in Africa edited by Firoze Manji and Stephen Marks. 2007. Fahamu / Pambazuka News

231 Wasserman, H. South Africa and China as BRICS Partners, Media Perspectives on Geopolitical Shifts. 2015. Journal of Asian and African Studies.

232 Pautasso, D. The Role of Africa in the New Maritime Silk Road. 2016. Brazilian Journal of African Studies. 1 (2). pp. 118-130.

233 Feng, E. and Pilling, D. The other side of Chinese investment in Africa. 27th March 2019. The Financial Times. https://www.ft.com/content/9f5736d8-14e1-11e9-a581-4ff78404524e [Accessed 4th November 2020

234 Ching, K. L. The Specter of Global China: Politics, Labor and Foreign Investment in Africa. 2018. University of Chicago Press. p2

235 Wasserman, H. South Africa and China as BRICS Partners.

236 BWI. Chinese MNCs in Africa. Building and Woodworkers International. 2016.

237 Marais, H, and Labuschagne, JP. China's role in African infrastructure and capital projects. 22nd March 2019. Deloitte. https://www2.deloitte.com/us/en/insights/industry/public-sector/china-investment-africa-infrastructure-development.html# [Accessed 4th November 2020]

238 Xinhua. Chinese firm signs agreement to manage Ethiopian industrial park. 31st May 2019. http://www.xinhuanet.com/english/2019-05/31/c_138103636.htm [Accessed 4th November 2020]

239 Bloomberg. China Makes Biggest South Africa Car Plant Investment In 40 Years. 30th August 2016. https://www.industryweek.com/leadership/growth-strategies/article/21979921/china-makes-biggest-south-africa-car-

240 plant-investment-in-40-years [Accessed 4th November 2020]

240 Xi, JJ., Gelb, S., Li, JW. And Zhao ZX. Adjusting to Rising Costs on Chinese Light Manufacturing. Center for New Structural Economics. December 2017.

241 Danneberg, P., Kim,Y. and Schiller,D. Chinese Special Economic Zones in Africa: a new species of globalization. African-East Asian Affairs: The China Monitor. Issue 2 June 2013.

242 Pairult, T. China in Africa: Phoenix nests versus Special Economic Zones. 2019.

243 Ibid

244 While only 20 Chinese SEZs have been certified, making it easy for Chinese companies to move abroad and obtain financing, by the end of 2017 MOFCOM data are reported to have identified 99 overseas zones, with a cumulative investment of US$30.7 billion. (Pairult 2019)

245 China's Economic Zones in Africa: Lots of Hype, Little Hope. 20th August 2015. https://www.chinafile.com/library/china-africa-project/chinas-special-economic-zones-africa-lots-hype-little-hope [Accessed 4th November 2020]

246 Rise and stall: China's stepping stone to nowhere. 8th April 2015. African Business Magazine. https://africanbusinessmagazine.com/uncategorised/rise-and-stall-chinas-stepping-stone-to-nowhere/ [Accessed 4th November 2020]

247 Pairult, T. China in Africa: Phoenix nests versus Special Economic Zones. 2019.

248 Ching, K. L. The Specter of Global China.

249 Feng, E. and Pilling, D. The other side of Chinese investment in Africa.

250 Dahir, A.L. These are the African countries not signed to China's Belt and Road project.30th September 2019. Quartz Africa. https://qz.com/africa/1718826/the-african-countries-not-signed-to-chinas-belt-and-road-plan/ [Accessed 4th November 2020]

251 Chad imposes U.S.$1.2bn fine on Chinese oil firm. 7th April 2014. The Economist. http://country.eiu.com/article.aspx?articleid=91702793&Country=Chad&topic=Economy&subtopic=+Forecast&subsubtopic=Policy+trends&u=1&pid=391399623&oid=391399623 [Accessed 4th November]

252 Chad successfully meets the challenge.: $815 million if financial commitment. 1st July 2019. Kapital Afrik. https://www.kapitalafrik.com/2019/07/01/chad-successfully-meets-the-challenge-815-million-of-financial-commitment/ [Accessed 4th November 2020].

253 Dahir, A.L. A legal tussel over a strategic African port sets up a challenge for China's Belt and Road plan. 28th February 2019. https://qz.com/africa/1560998/djibouti-dp-world-port-case-challenges-chinas-belt-and-road/ [Accessed 4th November 2020]

254 Breuer, J. Two Belts, One Road? The role of Africa in China's Belt and Road initiative. Blickwechsel. July 2017

255 Dahir, A.L. A legal tussel over a strategic African port sets up a challenge for China's Belt and Road plan

256 Cited in: Chinese army establishes first overseas base in Djibouti. 12th July 2017. The BRICS Post https://thebricspost.com/chinese-army-establishing-first-overseas-base-in-djibouti/ [Accessed 4th November 2020]

257 Ibid

258 Scott, E. China's Silk Road Strategy. A Foothold in the Suez but Looking to Israel. 10th October 2014. Jamestown Foundation. https://jamestown.org/program/chinas-silk-road-strategy-a-foothold-in-the-suez-but-looking-to-israel/ [Accessed 4th November 2020]

259 Peter, K. China and the 21st Century Maritime Silk Road. 16th March 2017. PAGEO Research Institute http://www.geopolitika.hu/en/2017/03/16/china-and-the-21st-century-new-maritime-silk-road/ [Accessed 4th November 2020]

260 Xinhua. Ghana begins commercial gas production in Chinese built plant. 3rd April 2015. China Daily. https://www.chinadaily.com.cn/world/2015-04/03/content_19996135.htm [Accessed 4th November 2020]

261 Smith, E. China's $2 billion deal with Ghana sparks fears over debt, influence and the environment. 21st November 2019. CNBC. https://www.cnbc.com/2019/11/21/chinas-2-billion-ghana-deal-fears-over-debt-influence-environment.html [Accessed 4th November 2020]

262 Herbling, D. and Li, DD. China's Built a Road to Nowhere in Kenya. 18th July 2019. https://www.bloomberg.com/news/features/2019-07-19/china-s-belt-and-road-leaves-kenya-with-a-railroad-to-nowhere [Accessed 4th November 2020]

263 China funds reconstruction of fishing port in Mozambique. 1st October 2014. Connecting to Mozambique. http://www.connectingtomocambique.com/nl/china-funds-reconstruction-of-fishing-port-in-mozambique/ [Accessed 4th November 2020]

264 Baker, L. Bridging Perceptions: China in Mozambique.27th August 2019. Marco Polo. https://macropolo.org/analysis/china-mozambique-elite-perceptions/ [Accessed 4th November 2020].

265 Mulyungi, P. Lekki deep sea port project in Nigeria receives US $221 funding from CHEC. https://constructionreviewonline.com/2020/05/nigerias-lekki-deep-sea-port-project-receives-equity-funding/ [Accessed 4th November 2020]

266 New Port in Lagos will be Chinese Financed, Chinese Built. 24th October 2019. The Maritime Executive. https://www.maritime-executive.com/article/china-finances-new-chinese-built-port-in-lagos-nigeria [Accessed 4th November 2020]

267 MOFCOM. Ogun-Guangdong Free Trade Zone. 12th July 2018. Ministry of Commerce. http://english.mofcom.gov.cn/article/newsrelease/counselorsoffice/westernasiaandafricare

268 Magubane, K. Mboweni on Eskom bail out: how China loan delay triggered a scramble for funds. 19th April 2019. https://www.news24.com/fin24/Economy/mboweni-on-eskom-bail-out-how-china-loan-delay-triggered-a-scramble-for-funds-20190419 [Accessed 6th November 2020]

269 Mhlanga, T. Brics bank fails to live up to hype. 22nd June 2018. Mail & Guardian. https://mg.co.za/article/2018-06-22-00-brics-bank-fails-to-live-up-to-hype/ [Accessed 6th November 2020]

270 Winning, A. China's Xi pledges US$14.7 billion investment on South Africa visit. 24th July 2018. Reuters. [Accessed 6th November 2020] https://www.reuters.com/article/us-safrica-china/chinas-xi-pledges-14-7-billion-investment-on-south-africa-visit-idUSKBN1KE2A3

271 Peter, K. China and the 21st Century Maritime Silk Road.

272 Cited in: 'Africa Rising' in Retreat. Patrick Bond. September 2017. Monthly Review.

273 Hursh, J. Tanzania Pushes Back on Chinese Port Project. 12th February 2019. The Maritime Executive https://www.maritime-executive.com/editorials/tanzania-pushes-back-on-chinese-port-project [Accessed 6th November 2020]

274 Kapembwa, J. China ready to revitalize Tazara railway project.19th August 2019. The Southern Times. https://southerntimesafrica.com/site/news/china-ready-to-revitalize-tazara-railway-project [Accessed 6th November 2020]

275 Ching, K. L. The Specter of Global China.

276 Chinese firm launches $832 million Zambia copper mine. 22nd August 2018. https://www.reuters.com/article/us-zambia-mining/chinese-firm-launches-832-million-zambia-copper-mine-idUSKCN1L71P7 [Accessed 6th November 2020]

277 Takouleu, J.M. Zambia: Sinohydro halts work at Kafue Gorge Dam site. 23rd September 2019. https://www.afrik21.africa/en/zambia-sinohydro-halts-work-at-kafue-gorge-dam-site/ [Accessed 6th November 2020]

278 Kapembwa, J. China ready to revitalize Tazara railway project.

279 Kapembwa, J. China ready to revitalize Tazara railway project.

280 Knowles, Daniel. The lunatic express, The Economist, August/September 2016. https://www.1843magazine.com/features/the-lunatic-express. [Accessed 6th November 2020]

281 The official website of EAC. EAC Railways sub-sector Projects. https://www.eac.int/infrastructure/railways-transport-sub-sector/92-sector/infrastructure/railways. [Accessed 6th November 2020]

282 中华人民共和国中央人民政府网站．蒙内铁路 通向美好未来，August 13, 2018. http://www.gov.cn/xinwen/2018-08/13/content_5313422.htm. [Accessed 6th November 2020]

283 中非合作论坛．肯尼亚蒙内铁路中国建设者回击抹黑中非合作言论，April 11, 2018. https://www.fmprc.gov.cn/zflt/chn/zxxx/t1549871.htm. [Accessed 6th November 2020]

284 中华人民共和国中央人民政府网站．蒙内铁路 通向美好未来，August 13, 2018. http://www.gov.cn/xinwen/2018-08/13/content_5313422.htm. [Accessed 6th November 2020]

285 新华社．习近平主席特使、国务委员王勇出席肯尼亚蒙内铁路通车仪式，May 31, 2017. http://www.xinhuanet.com//politics/2017-05/31/c_1121064853.htm. [Accessed 6th November 2020]

286 吕强．蒙内铁路助力肯尼亚经济发展，人民日报，November 12, 2018. http://paper.people.com.cn/rmrb/html/2018-11/12/nw.D110000renmrb_20181112_4-21.htm.

287 Freytas-Tamura, Kimiko. 中资建造的天价铁路，肯尼亚人感叹太疯狂，纽约时报中文网，June 9, 2017. [Accessed 6th November 2020] https://cn.nytimes.com/world/20170609/kenyans-fear-chinese-backed-railway-is-another-lunatic-express/.

288 Adama, Joe. EXCLUSIVE: How Italian Firm Was Shut Out Of Kenya's SGR Project, The Star, June 21, 2014. https://www.the-star.co.ke/news/2014/06/21/exclusive-how-italian-firm-was-shut-out-of-kenyas-sgr-project_c956617

289 Akwiri, Joseph. Kenya charges three Chinese railway workers with bribery, Reuters, November 26, 2018. https://www.reuters.com/article/us-kenya-china-crime/kenya-charges-three-chinese-railway-workers-with-bribery-idUSKCN1NV1TI [Accessed 6th November 2020]

290 中华人民共和国商务部．中肯合作筑就蒙内铁路，"一带一路"在非开花结果，June 1, 2017. http://www.mofcom.gov.cn/article/i/jyjl/k/201706/20170602584382.shtml. [Accessed 14th June 2019]

291 Walfula, Paul. Exclusive: Behind the SGR walls, Standard Digital, July 08, 2018. https://www.standardmedia.co.ke/article/2001287119/exclusive-behind-the-sgr-walls. [Accessed 6th November 2020]

292 Okoth, Edwin. SGR pact with China a risk to Kenyan sovereignty, assets, Daily Nation, January 13, 2019. https://allafrica.com/stories/201901140451.html [Accessed 6th November 2020]

293 新华社．中国路桥与肯尼亚铁路公司签署蒙内铁路运维合同，May 30, 2017. http://www.xinhuanet.com/2017-05/30/c_1121058860.htm. [Accessed 6th November 2020]

294 Obiorah, N. Who's Afraid of China in Africa? Towards an African Civil Society Perspective on China–Africa Relations. African perspectives on China in Africa. 2007. Networks for Social Justice.

295 Frankopan, P. (2019). The New Silk Roads: The Present and Future of the World. London: Bloomsbury.

296 The data was released to support the Debt Service Suspension Initiative of G20 countries to ease the impact of

the Covid-19 pandemic.

297 Huang, YF. and Brautigam, D. Putting a Dollar Amount on China's Loans to the Developing World. 24th June 2020. The Diplomat. https://thediplomat.com/2020/06/putting-a-dollar-amount-on-chinas-loans-to-the-developing-world/ [Accessed 6th November 2020]

298 Sun, Y. China's Aid to Africa: Monster or Messiah? 7th February 2014. Brookings. https://www.brookings.edu/opinions/chinas-aid-to-africa-monster-or-messiah/ [Accessed 6th November 2020]

299 Olander, E. China's infrastructure model is changing. Here's how. 14th January 2020. The Africa Report. Accessed 6th November 2020 https://www.theafricareport.com/22133/chinas-infrastructure-finance-model-is-changing-heres-how/ [Accessed 6th November 2020]

300 Sun, Y. China's Aid to Africa: Monster or Messiah?

301 Nyabiage, J. How Chinese loans can become 'perilous pitfalls' for Africa. 8th March 2020. https://www.scmp.com/news/china/diplomacy/article/3073993/how-chinese-loans-can-become-perilous-pitfalls-africa [Accessed 6th November 2020]

302 Ching, K. L. The Specter of Global China pp.47-48

303 Magubane, K. Don't panic over Eskom 's Chinese loans, says Zambian economist. 4th February 2019. https://www.fin24.com/Special-Reports/Mining-Indaba/dont-panic-over-eskoms-chinese-loans-says-zambian-economist-20190204 [Accessed 6th November 2020]

304 Servant, J.C. China steps in as Zambia runs out of loan options. 11th December 2019. The Guardian. https://www.theguardian.com/global-development/2019/dec/11/china-steps-in-as-zambia-runs-out-of-loan-options [Accessed 6th November 2020]

305 Obiorah, N. Who's Afraid of China in Africa? Towards an African Civil Society Perspective on China-Africa Relations. In: African perspectives on China in Africa. 2007. Networks for Social Justice.

306 Africa and China: then and now. Interview with Kwesi Kwaa. In: African perspectives on China in Africa. 2007. Networks for Social Justice..

307 Kuo, L Beijing is cultivating the next generation of African leaders by training them in China. 14th December 2017. Quartz Africa. https://qz.com/africa/1119447/china-is-training-africas-next-generation-of-leaders/ [Accessed 6th November 2020]

308 China donates US$146 million to build infrastructure in Sao Tome and Principe. 26th April 2017. https://macauhub.com.mo/2017/04/26/china-doa-146-milhoes-de-dolares-para-construcao-de-infra-estruturas-em-sao-tome-e-principe/ [Accessed 6th November 2020]

309 Maasho, A. China denies report it attacked African Union headquarters. 29th January 2018. https://www.reuters.com/article/us-africanunion-summit-china/china-denies-report-it-hacked-african-union-headquarters-idUSKBN1FI2I5 [Accessed 6th November 2020]

310 Lau, C. Jailed ex-Hong Kong official Patrick Ho released after finishing US sentence for bribery and money laundering . 9th June 2020. https://www.scmp.com/news/hong-kong/law-and-crime/article/3088112/jailed-ex-hong-kong-official-patrick-ho-set-be [Accessed 6th November 2020]

311 Burgis, T. Queensway Group probed over use of 'secrecy jurisdictions'. 4th May 2015. https://www.ft.com/content/a95e8252-f015-11e4-ab73-00144feab7de [Accessed 6th November 2020]

312 The Chinese in Africa. April 20th 2011. The Economist. http://www.economist.com/node/18586448/ [Accessed 6th November 2020]

313 In: Chinese MNCs in Africa: Development Burden on Labour: Political, Economic and Cultural Perspectives. 2016. Building and Woodworkers International.

314 Ching, K. L. The Specter of Global China. p62

315 Pilling, D. It is wrong to demonise Chinese labour practices in Africa. 3rd July 2019. https://www.ft.com/content/6326dc9a-9cb8-11e9-9c06-a4640c9feebb [Accessed 6th November 2020]

316 Breuer, J. Two Belts, One Road? The role of Africa in China's Belt and Road initiative.

317 Bond, P. 'Africa rising' in retreat: Signs of new resistances.

318 Ryder, H. African countries want more "win" from the win-win , but China isn't quite ready.7th September 2018. https://qz.com/africa/1382074/what-african-countries-really-get-from-focac-china-summit/

319 Sinosure provides payment guarantee or default insurance for many BRI projects.

320 Ng, E. Botched Chinese railway project in Africa is a warning to Belt and Road investors. 29th October 2018. South China Morning Post. https://www.scmp.com/business/banking-finance/article/2170549/botched-chinese-railway-project-africa-warning-belt-and [Accessed 6th November 2020]

321 This section is somewhat based on the report, "Patterns, Practices and Implications of Chinese Investment in Asia: A Critical Perspective", written for the Asian Transnational Corporations Monitoring Network (forthcoming).

322 Kamal, M., Li, Z., Bashir, M., Khan, K., Ashraf, B. and Shaikh, S. (2014). Trend and Determinants of China's OFDI in Asia. Journal of Economics and Sustainable Development. Vol. 5, No.22. pp110-121.

323 Eurostat. (2017). World direct investment patterns. Available from: https://ec.europa.eu/eurostat/statistics-explained/index.php/World_direct_investment_patterns#Statistics_on_foreign_direct_investment [Accessed 12. April 2018].

324 Salidianova, N. and Koch-Weser, J. (2015). China's

Economic Ties with ASEAN: A Country-by-Country Analysis. U.S.-China Economic and Security Review Commission.

325 Ibid

326 Khokhar, T. (2017). Where does Chinese development finance go? The World Bank. http://blogs.worldbank.org/opendata/where-does-chinese-development-finance-go [Accessed 8th December 2018]

327 These loans had not necessarily been disbursed.

328 Kynge, J. and Yu, S. China faces wave of calls for debt relief of 'Belt and Road' projects. 30th April 2020. The Financial Times. https://www.ft.com/content/5a3192be-27c6-4fe7-87e7-78d4158bd39b [Accessed 6th November 2020]

329 Ibid

330 AidData. (2017). China's Global Development Footprint. https://www.aiddata.org/china-official-finance [Accessed 8. Dec.2018].

331 China Power n.d. Does China dominate global investment? Center for Strategic and International Studies. https://chinapower.csis.org/china-foreign-direct-investment/ [Accessed 11. Dec. 2018].

332 Franceschini, I. (2017). Outsourcing Exploitation: Chinese and Cambodian Garment Workers Compared. Made in China, Issue 3. 2017.

333 Miller, T. (2017). China's Asian Dream: Empire Building Along the New Silk Road. London: Zed Books.

334 Frankopan, P. (2019). The New Silk Roads: The Present and Future of the World. London: Bloomsbury.

335 Miller, T. (2017). China's Asian Dream

336 Shi, J. and Churchill, O. (2018). US Competes with China's US$113 million Asian investment programme. South China Morning Post. [online]. https://www.scmp.com/news/china/economy/article/2157381/us-competes-chinas-belt-and-road-initiative-new-asian-investment [Accessed 11. Dec. 2018].

337 Reuters (2018). Australia, Japan join US infrastructure push in Asia. [online]. Available from: https://www.cnbc.com/2018/07/31/australia-japan-join-us-infrastructure-push-in-asia.html [Accessed 11. Dec. 2018].

338 He, Y. (2014). China's overcapacity crisis can spur growth through overseas expansion. South China Morning Post. [online]. https://www.scmp.com/comment/insight-opinion/article/1399681/chinas-overcapacity-crisis-can-spur-growth-through-overseas [Accessed 18. Dec. 2018].

339 Ongdee, S. (2016). Thailand's Eastern Economic Corridor the New Great Hope: The Nation Columnist. The Straits Times. [online]. https://www.straitstimes.com/asia/se-asia/thailands-eastern-economic-corridor-the-great-new-hope-the-nation-columnist [Accessed 18. Dec. 2018].

340 Pan, M. (2017). High-speed rail project finally gets on track. China Daily. [online]. Available from: http://www.chinadaily.com.cn/a/201712/22/WS5a3c4675a31008cf16da2bdc.html [Accessed 18. Dec. 2018].

341 Chan, S. (2018). Chinese investment welcomed but with proper regulation. Khmer Times. [online]. Available from: https://www.khmertimeskh.com/50526190/chinese-investment-welcomed-but-with-proper-regulation/ [Accessed 18. Dec. 2018].

342 Wright, G. (2018). Anti-Chinese Sentiment on the Rise in Cambodia. The Diplomat. [online]. Available from: https://thediplomat.com/2018/11/anti-chinese-sentiment-on-the-rise-in-cambodia/ [Accessed 18. Dec. 2018].

343 Markey, D. and West, J. (2016). Behind China's Gambit in Pakistan. Council on Foreign Relations. [online]. Available from: https://www.cfr.org/expert-brief/behind-chinas-gambit-pakistan [Accessed 18. Dec. 2018].

344 Husain, K. (2016). IMF warns of looming CPEC bill. Dawn. [online]. Available from: https://www.dawn.com/news/1290523 [Accessed 18. Dec. 2018].

345 Hurley, J., Morris, S. and Portelance, G. (2018). Examining the Debt Implications of the Belt and Road Initiative from a Policy Perspective. Center for Global Development. Policy Paper 121. March 2018.

346 As a result of protest the exact percentage stake ceded to China was lowered from 80% to 70%, although this still means de facto control.

347 Unrepayable debt is nevertheless a significant risk to China, even where payment is to be made in natural resources, as the case of Venezuela shows.

348 Chellaney, B. (2018). China's Debt Trap Diplomacy. Project Syndicate. [online]. Available from: https://www.project-syndicate.org/commentary/china-one-belt-one-road-loans-debt-by-brahma-chellaney-2017-01?g [Accessed 13. Dec. 2018].

349 Nachemson, A. A Chinese colony takes shape in Cambodia. 5th June 2018. Asia Times. https://asiatimes.com/2018/06/a-chinese-colony-takes-shape-in-cambodia/ Accessed 6th November 2020]

350 USIP. (2018). China's Role in Myanmar's Internal Conflicts. United States Institute for Peace. [online]. Available from: https://www.usip.org/publications/2018/09/chinas-role-myanmars-internal-conflicts [Accessed 19. Dec. 2018].

351 Xinhua. (2015). Interview: Diplomat denies Chinese involvement in conflict in northern Myanmar. Xinhua. [online]. Available from: http://www.xinhuanet.com/english/china/2015-02/25/c_127517919.htm [Accessed 19. Dec. 2018].

352 Chan, A. (2011). Hired on Sufferance: China's Migrant Workers in Singapore. China Labour Bulletin.

353 Kow, G. C., and Wong, A. (2017). Broken Dreams-The Plight of Forest City Migrant Workers. Malaysiakini [online]. Available from: https://m.malaysiakini.com/news/381555 [Accessed 19. Dec. 2018].

354 Markey, D. and West, J. (2016). Behind China's Gambit in Pakistan. Council on Foreign Relations. [online]. Available from: https://www.cfr.org/expert-brief/behind-chinas-gambit-pakistan [Accessed 18. Dec. 2018].

355 Amnesty International. (2015). Myanmar: Letpadaung mine protesters still demand justice. Amnesty International. Available from: https://www.amnesty.org/en/latest/news/2015/11/myanmar-letpadaung-mine-protesters-still-denied-justice/ [Accessed 19. Dec. 2018].

356 Markey, D. and West, J. (2016). Behind China's Gambit in Pakistan.

357 Pearl, H. (2018). China-backed hydroelectric dam threatens world's rarest orangutan. AFP. Available from: https://www.hongkongfp.com/author/afp/ [Accessed 19. Dec. 2018].

358 Karokaro, A. (2017). Protest against hydropower plant in Sumatra ends with injuries. Mongabay. Available from: https://news.mongabay.com/2017/09/protest-against-hydropower-plant-in-sumatra-ends-with-injuries/ [Accessed 19. Dec. 2018].

359 人民网．瓜达尔港——中巴经济走廊的璀璨明珠，光明日报，August 26, 2018. http://world.people.com.cn/n1/2018/0826/c1002-30251676.html. [Accessed February 10, 2019]

360 Anonymous. Gwadar port: 'history-making milestones', Dawn, April 14, 2008. https://www.dawn.com/news/297994/gwadar-port-history-making-milestones.

361 The official website of SASAC. 中交股份承建的巴基斯坦瓜达尔港开港，March 22, 2007. http://www.sasac.gov.cn/n2588025/n2588124/c4023232/content.html. [Accessed February 10, 2019]

362 胡世龙．瓜达尔港"一波三折"建设路，国际金融报，April 20, 2015. http://paper.people.com.cn/gjjrb/html/2015-04/20/content_1555581.htm. [Accessed February 10, 2019]

363 Anonymous. 3 engineers killed in car bomb in Pakistan, China Daily, May 03, 2004. http://www.chinadaily.com.cn/english/doc/2004-05/03/content_328070.htm. [Accessed February 10, 2019]

364 Anonymous. 13 held on charge of killing 3 Chinese: Gwadar bomb attack, Dawn, May 05, 2004. https://www.dawn.com/news/393852. [Accessed February 10, 2019]

365 Anonymous. Gwadar port: 'history-making milestones', Dawn, April 14, 2008. https://www.dawn.com/news/297994/gwadar-port-history-making-milestones. [Accessed February 10, 2019]

366 Khan, Zia. Singapore port operator on way out of Gwadar, The Express Tribune, August 09, 2012. https://tribune.com.pk/story/419578/singapore-port-operator-on-way-out-of-gwadar/. [Accessed 6th November 2020]

367 BR Research. The mysterious China Overseas Ports Holding Company, Business Recorder, February 19, 2018. https://www.brecorder.com/2018/02/19/399768/the-mysterious-china-overseas-ports-holding-company/. [Accessed 6th November 2020]

368 中国政府网．李克强在巴基斯坦议会发表演讲 积极评价中巴友谊，新华社，May 23, 2013. http://www.gov.cn/ldhd/2013-05/23/content_2410135.htm. [Accessed February 10, 2019]

369 Anonymous. Chinese firm awarded Rs55bn power project at Gwadar, Dawn, March 31, 2017. https://www.dawn.com/news/1336376 [Accessed 6th November 2020]

370 新浪财经．中交建签约巴基斯坦快速路项目 瓜达尔港优势将扩大，二十一世纪经济报道，September 26, 2017. http://finance.sina.com.cn/chanjing/gsnews/2017-09-26/doc-ifymenmt7064459.shtml. [Accessed February 10, 2019]

371 Lee, Robin. An introduction to the China-Pakistan Economic Corridor, Borderless Movement, August 16, 2017. https://borderless-hk.com/2017/08/16/an-introduction-to-the-china-pakistan-economic-corridor/. [Accessed February 10, 2019]

372 Ibid.

373 Ebrahim, Zofeen. What's happening at Pakistan's Gwadar port?, China Dialogue, June 16, 2017. https://www.chinadialogue.net/article/show/single/en/9869-What-s-happening-at-Pakistan-s-Gwadar-port-. [Accessed February 10, 2019]

374 Anonymous. Chinese camp in Gwadar attacked, Dawn, November 16, 2005. https://www.dawn.com/news/165799. [Accessed February 10, 2019]

375 Yousafzai, Gul. Attack on workers at key Pakistan port for Chinese project; 26 hurt, Reuters, October 20, 2017. https://www.reuters.com/article/us-pakistan-attacks/attack-on-workers-at-key-pakistan-port-for-chinese-project-26-hurt-idUSKBN1CP0O6. [Accessed February 10, 2019]

376 Janjua, Haroon; Shams, Shamil. China consulate attack: Why Pakistan's Baloch separatists are against Beijing, Deutsche Welle, November 23, 2018. https://www.dw.com/en/china-consulate-attack-why-pakistans-baloch-separatists-are-against-beijing/a-46424112. [Accessed 10th November 2020]

377 Notezai, Muhammad. Why Balochs Are Targeting China, The Diplomat, November 26, 2018. https://thediplomat.com/2018/11/why-balochs-are-targeting-china/. [Accessed 10th November 2020]

378 Ibid.

379 Hillman, Jonathan. Game of Loans: How China Bought Hambantota, CSIS, April 2, 2018. https://www.csis.org/analysis/game-loans-how-china-bought-hambantota. [Accessed 10th November 2020]

380 Ibid.

381 Abi-habib. How China Got Sri Lanka to Cough Up a Port, The New York Times, June 25, 2018. https://www.nytimes.com/2018/06/25/world/asia/china-sri-lanka-port.html. [Accessed 10th November 2020]

382 The official website of MMS. http://www.

mackinnonshipping.com/.

383 Sri Lanka Ports Authority. Development of Port in Hambantota. https://web.archive.org/web/20100306074012/http://www.slpa.lk/port_hambantota.asp?chk=4. [Accessed 10th November 2020]

384 Koh King Kee. 斯里兰卡汉班托塔港问题的真相，北京周报，September 29, 2018. http://www.beijingreview.com.cn/shishi/201809/t20180929_800143048.html. [Accessed 10th November 2020]

385 Ibid.

386 Anonymous. 中交建签署汉班托塔港口工程二期合同，一财网，January 4, 2011. https://www.yicai.com/news/643947.html. [Accessed 10th November 2020]

387 沈秋. "一带一路"项目 汉班托塔港连接东西方的航运中心，中国网，April 19, 2017. http://ydyl.china.com.cn/2017-04/19/content_40649949.htm [Accessed 10th November 2020]

388 Anonymous. 斯里兰卡汉班托塔港，光明日报，January 26, 2018. http://epaper.gmw.cn/gmrb/html/2018-01/26/nw.D110000gmrb_20180126_5-12.htm. [Accessed 10th November 2020]

389 Anonymous. 聚焦｜漢班托塔港「債務陷阱」老調重彈，斯里蘭卡前總統親筆回擊，壹讀，July 04, 2018. https://read01.com/zh-hk/Bn3PB8j.html#.XFnKQ1wzbIU. [Accessed 10th November 2020]

390 Koh King Kee. 斯里兰卡汉班托塔港问题的真相

391 Hillman, Jonathan. Game of Loans: How China Bought Hambantota

392 Abi-habib. How China Got Sri Lanka to Cough Up a Port, The New York Times, June 25, 2018. https://www.nytimes.com/2018/06/25/world/asia/china-sri-lanka-port.html. [Accessed 10th November 2020]

393 Ng, E. (2018). Chinese firms working on belt and road projects at risk of international disputes, say lawyers. South China Morning Post. Available from: https://www.scmp.com/business/companies/article/2148844/chinese-firms-working-belt-and-road-projects-risk-international [Accessed 19. Dec. 2018].

394 Pham, S. (2018). Malaysia halts a big China backed infrastructure project. CNN Business. Available from: https://money.cnn.com/2018/07/05/news/economy/malaysia-china-rail-project-suspended/index.html [Accessed 20. Dec. 2018].

395 Ibid

396 This section is adapted from Globalization Monitor's report: Chinese Investment in Germany: A preliminary investigation and report on our visit to Germany published in May 2019. Globalization Monitor would like to that Forum Arbeitswelten in Germany for its support with this research.

397 This is actually a decline in position from second place if only data from 2000-2014 is included. See Hanemann, T. and Huotari, M. (2016). A new record year for Chinese outbound investment in Europe. Mercator Institute for Chinese Studies and Rhodium Group.

398 Hanemann, T. and Huotari, M. (2015). Preparing for a new era of Chinese capital: Chinese FDI in Europe and Germany. Mercator Institute for Chinese Studies and Rhodium Group.

399 Fernández, E. (2018). Once welcoming, why Germany is wary of Chinese investment amid Trump's trade war. 26th August 2018. South China Morning Post. https://www.scmp.com/week-asia/business/article/2160911/once-welcoming-why-germany-wary-chinese-investment-amid-trumps [Accessed 10th November 2020]

400 Reuters. Chinese FDI into North America, Europe falls 73% in 2018: report. Reuters. 14th January 2019. https://www.reuters.com/article/us-china-fdi/chinese-fdi-into-north-america-europe-falls-73-percent-in-2018-report-idUSKCN1P800H [Accessed 10th November 2020]

401 Our visit took us to several cities including Cologne, Bochum, Düsseldorf, Duisburg and Monheim am Rhein.

402 Hamburg Marketing At home in the world. Hamburg Marketing. https://marketing.hamburg.de/internationality.html [Accessed 10th November 2020]

403 Deutsche Welle (Exit the Dragon? Chinese Investment in Germany. DW. 5th February 2018. https://www.dw.com/en/exit-the-dragon-chinese-investment-in-germany/a-42457712 [Accessed 10th November 2020]

404 Bian, SW. and Emons, O. (2017). Chinese investments in Germany: increasing in line with Chinese industrial policy. In: Chinese investments in Europe: corporate strategies and labour relations. Edited by Jan Drahokoupil. European Trade Union Initiative. Brussels.

405 Hanemann, T. and Huotari, M. (2015). Preparing for a new era of Chinese capital.

406 Ibid

407 Ibid

408 Ibid

409 German Chancellor Angela Merkel has recently described the BRI as an "important project" and commented that, "We, as Europeans, want to play an active part and that must lead to certain reciprocity…. We are seeing the project as a good visualization of interaction, interrelation and interdependence". Escobar, P. The EU bows to 'systemic rival' China. 27th March 2019. Asia Times. https://www.asiatimes.com/2019/03/article/the-eu-bows-to-systemic-rival-china/ [Accessed 10th November 2020]

410 Fernández, E. (2018). Once welcoming, why Germany is wary of Chinese investment amid Trump's trade war.

411 Bian, SW. and Emons, O. (2017). Chinese investments in Germany: increasing in line with Chinese industrial policy.

412 Hanemann, T. and Huotari, M. (2015). Preparing for a new era of Chinese capital.

413 Goetker, U. and Ningelgen, A. An update on foreign

investment control in Germany. McDermott Will and Emergy. https://www.mwe.com/insights/an-update-on-foreign-investment-control-in-germany/ [Accessed 10th November 2020]

414 Fernández, E. (2018). Once welcoming, why Germany is wary of Chinese investment amid Trump's trade war.

415 Whittaker, Z. US threatens to reduce intelligence sharing if Germany doesn't ban Huawei. TechCrunch. https://techcrunch.com/2019/03/11/germany-intelligence-sharing/ [Accessed 10th November 2020]

416 Deutsche Welle Exit the Dragon? Chinese Investment in Germany. DW. 5th February 2018. https://www.dw.com/en/exit-the-dragon-chinese-investment-in-germany/a-42457712 [Accessed 10th November 2020]

417 Hong Kong has long received by far the largest proportion of mainland Chinese ODI. In 2016, for instance, Hong Kong accounted for 58% of China's total ODI stocks according to official statistics. While some of this capital invested in Hong Kong is intended for reinvestment in mainland China, a significant proportion is also widely believed to be being redirected and invested overseas.

418 ETUI (Workplace representation. European Trade Union Initiative. https://www.worker-participation.eu/National-Industrial-Relations/Countries/Germany/Workplace-Representation/ [Accessed 10th November 2020]

419 Bian, SW. and Emons, O. (2017). Chinese investments in Germany: increasing in line with Chinese industrial policy.

420 World Steel Association. (2018). World Steel in Figures 2018. World Steel Association. Brussels.

421 KHD. KHD plans headcount reduction. KHD Humboldt Wedag. 12th March 2019. http://www.khd.com/ad-hoc-disclosure-details/items/khd-plans-headcount-reduction.html [Accessed 10th November 2020]

422 Bian, SW. (2018) Personalabbau in Chinesche Kontrollierten Unternehmen: Chinesische Investitionen in Deutschland. Mitbestimmungsreport Nr. 46. October 2018. Institut für Mitbestimmung und Unternehmensführung (I.M.U.) der Hans-Böckler-Stiftung.

423 Oltermann, P. Germany's 'China City': how Duisburg became Xi Jinping's gateway to Europe. 1st August 2018. The Guardian. https://www.theguardian.com/cities/2018/aug/01/germanys-china-city-duisburg-became-xi-jinping-gateway-europe [Accessed 10th November 2020] Xinhua (2018). New Silk Road brings more than trade to China, Europe. 18th August 2018. Xinhua. http://www.xinhuanet.com/english/2018-08/18/c_137399857.htm [Accessed 10th November 2020]

424 Chazon. G. The unlikely end to China's new silk road is in Germany's Rust Belt. 10th April 2019. Ozy and the Financial Times. https://www.ozy.com/fast-forward/the-unlikely-end-to-chinas-new-silk-road-is-in-germanys-rust-belt/93751 [Accessed 10th November 2020]

425 Oltermann, P. Germany's 'China City'

426 Xinhua New Silk Road brings more than trade to China, Europe.

427 Grey, J. and Schlautmann, C. How China put Duisburg back on the Trade Map. Handelsblatt Today. 15th August 2018. https://www.handelsblatt.com/today/companies/the-freight-game-how-china-put-duisburg-back-on-the-trade-map/23583018.html?ticket=ST-460524-IdCD0S2zDuNqEvadZZ4c-ap5 [Accessed 10th November 2020]

428 Ibid

429 Cited in: Chazon. G. (2019). The unlikely end to China's new silk road is in Germany's Rust Belt.
430 World Shipping Council Top 50 World Container Ports. World Shipping Council. http://www.worldshipping.org/about-the-industry/global-trade/top-50-world-container-ports [Accessed April 15th 2019]

431 HHLA (Combined Management Report. HHLA Annual Report 2017. Hamburg Hafen und Logistik AG.

432 HHLA How CTA works. Hamburg Hafen Und Logistik AG. https://hhla.de/en/container/cta/how-cta-works.html [Accessed April 15th 2019]

433 Foster, N. HafenCity scheme set to transform Hamburg's property market. 12th April 2014. The Financial Times. https://www.ft.com/content/5dc98988-bb35-11e3-948c-00144feabdc0 [Accessed 10th November 2020]

434 Cited in: World Maritime News. Cargo throughput declines at Port of Hamburg. World Maritime News. 21st May 2018. Available from: https://worldmaritimenews.com/archives/253179/cargo-throughput-declines-at-port-of-hamburg/ [Accessed 10th November 2020]

435 CCCC is a publicly traded company listed on the Hong Kong stock exchange (SEHK: 1800) since 2006 and on the Shanghai stock exchange (SSE: 601800) since 2012.

436 Louppova, J. Chinese consortium to build a new container terminal in Hamburg? 21st July 2017. port.today. https://port.today/cccc-builds-container-terminal-hamburg/

437 Schlautmann, C. (Chinese land chunk of Hamburg's Port. Handelsblatt Today. https://global.handelsblatt.com/companies/chinese-land-chunk-of-hamburgs-port-797845 [Accessed 10th November 2020]

438 Ibid

439 Xinhua. China signs MOUs with 37 African countries, AU on B&R development. 7th September 2018. http://www.xinhuanet.com/english/2018-09/07/c_137452482.htm [Accessed 16th November 2020]

440 Frankopan, P. (2019). The New Silk Roads: The Present and Future of the World. London: Bloomsbury.

441 Ibid

442 For instance, it has been suggested that European trade unions seek to establish contact with Chinese company unions after a company is taken over by a Chinese company,

particularly state-owned companies, as a way to better represent employee interests in China. (See: Wolfgang Muller. Annex. Chinese investors: what do works councils and trade unions need to be aware of ? In: Chinese investment in Europe: corporate strategies and labour relations. Edited by Jan Drahokoupil. 2017. European Trade Union Initiative).

443 Hu, WJ. Myanmar should regulate labor unions to help attract more Chinese investment. 27th February 2017. Global Times. http://www.globaltimes.cn/content/1034995.shtml [Accessed 16th November 2020]

444 Kow, G. C., and Wong, A. Broken Dreams-The Plight of Forest City Migrant Workers. 8th May 2017. Malaysiakini. https://m.malaysiakini.com/news/381555 [Accessed 19th December 2018].
445 Chinese Workers' Labour Dispute in Saipan Exposes Major Issues in Chinese Overseas Investment. 13th September 2017. Hong Kong Confederation of Trade Unions. https://en.hkctu.org.hk/node/187 [Accessed 30th November 2020].

Lau, M. 'If we go home now, we'll die': Chinese couple in Saipan back-pay row vow to fight on despite US labour deal. 7th March 2018. South China Morning Post. https://www.scmp.com/news/china/diplomacy-defence/article/2136014/if-we-go-home-now-well-die-chinese-couple-saipan-back [Accessed 30th November 2020]

446 Zhao, L. China has proposed 3 marine passages for Belt and Road. 23rd June 2017. China Daily Europe. http://europe.chinadaily.com.cn/epaper/2017-06/23/content_29856822.htm [Accessed 23rd November 2020]

447 Frankopan, P. (2019). The New Silk Roads.

448 Lee, R. An introduction the China-Pakistan Economic Corridor. 16th August 2017. Borderless Movement https://borderless-hk.com/2017/08/16/an-introduction-to-the-china-pakistan-economic-corridor/ [Accessed 23rd November 2020]

449 Lindsay, S. China-Laos railway marred by compensation issues and pollution. 11th June 2019. ASEAN Today. https://www.aseantoday.com/2019/06/china-laos-railway-marred-by-compensation-issues-and-pollution/ [Accessed 9th November 2020]

450 Ives, M. China's Belt and Road Initiative Threatens to Pave the Planet. 16th December 2019. Sierra. https://www.sierraclub.org/sierra/2020-1-january-february/feature/chinas-belt-and-road-initiative-threatens-pave-planet [Accessed 23rd November 2020]

451 Urban, F. and Nordensvard, J. (2014). China Dams the World: The Environmental and Social Impact of Chinese Dams, E-International Relations.

452 Ibid

453 Vision and Actions on Jointly Building Silk Road Economic Belt and 21st Century Maritime Silk Road. National Development and Reform Commission, Ministry of Foreign Affairs and Ministry of Commerce of the People's Republic of China. March 2015.

454 Feng, H. China's Belt and Road Initiative Still Pushing Coal. 2017. Chinadialogue. https://www.chinadialogue.net/article/show/single/en/9785-China-s-Belt-and-Road-Initiative-still- pushing-coal [Accessed 19th December 2018].
455 Allen-Ebrahimian, B. Russia Is the Biggest Recipient of Chinese Foreign Aid. 11th October 2017. Foreign Policy. https://foreignpolicy.com/2017/10/11/russia-is-the-biggest-recipient-of-chinese- foreign-aid-north-korea/ [Accessed 19th December 2018].

456 Jiang, F. Saudi Arabia joins CPEC with an investment of USD 10 bln. 26th September 2018. Xinhua Silk Road Information. Service. https://eng.yidaiyilu.gov.cn/qwyw/rdxw/67201.htm [Accessed 19th December 2018].

457 Makortoff, K. China slammed as EM firms accused of 'pathetic transparency levels. 11th July 2016. CNBC. https://www.cnbc.com/2016/07/11/china-slammed-as-em-firms-accused-of-pathetic-transparency-levels.html [Accessed 23rd November 2020]

458 Weinland, D. China to tackle corruption in Belt and Road projects. 18th July 2019. Financial Times. https://www.ft.com/content/a5815e66-a91b-11e9-984c-fac8325aaa04 [Accessed 9th December 2020]

459 Sanderson, H. and Forsythe, M. China's Superbank: Debt, Oil and Influence — How China Development Bank is Rewriting the Rules of Finance. 2013. Singapore: Bloomberg
 Morambudali, U. Is Sri Lanka Really a Victim of China's Debt Trap? 14th May 2019. The Diplomat. https://thediplomat.com/2019/05/is-sri-lanka-really-a-victim-of-chinas-debt-trap/ [Accessed 23rd November 2020]

460 Morambudali, U. Is Sri Lanka Really a Victim of China's Debt Trap? 14th May 2019. The Diplomat. https://thediplomat.com/2019/05/is-sri-lanka-really-a-victim-of-chinas-debt-trap/ [Accessed 23rd November 2020]

461 Frankopan, P. (2019). The New Silk Roads.
Alarm in Kenya over risk of Chinese "takeover" of Mombasa port. 8th January 2019. Global Construction Review. https://www.globalconstructionreview.com/news/alarm-kenya-over-risk-chinese-takeover-mombasa-por/ [Accessed 23rd November 2020]

462 Mutethya, E. Kenya and China dismiss Mombasa port takeover rumours. 8th January 2019. China Daily. http://www.chinadaily.com.cn/a/201901/08/WS5c343d6ca31068606745f7f5.html [Accessed 23rd November 2020]

463 Cited in: Greenfield, C. and Barrett, J. Tonga PM fears asset seizures as Pacific debts to China mount. 16th August 2018. Reuters. https://www.reuters.com/article/us-pacific-debt-tonga-graphic/tonga-pm-fears-asset-seizures-as-pacific-debts-to-china-mount-idUSKBN1L10KM [Accessed 23rd November 2020]

464 Tonga gets five years' grace on Chinese loan as Pacific nation joins Belt and Road Initiative. 18th November 2018. ABC NEWS. https://www.abc.net.au/news/2018-11-19/china-defers-tongas-loan-payments-as-nation-signs-up-to-bri/10509140 [Accessed 23rd November 2020]

465 Horton, C. El Salvador Recognizes China in Blow to Taiwan. 21st August 2018. The New York Times. https://www.

nytimes.com/2018/08/21/world/asia/taiwan-el-salvador-diplomatic-ties.html [Accessed 23rd November 2020]

466 Yu, J.M. and Blanchard, B. Taiwan says China dangles $3 billion to grab ally Dominican Republic. 30th April 2018. Reuters. https://www.reuters.com/article/us-china-dominicanrepublic-taiwan/taiwan-says-china-dangled-3-billion-to-grab-ally-dominican-republic-idUSKBN1I22LN [Accessed 23rd November 2020]

467 Peter, K. China and the 21st Century Maritime Silk Road. 16th March 2017. PAGEO Research Institute. http://www.geopolitika.hu/en/2017/03/16/china-and-the-21st-century-new-maritime-silk-road/ [Accessed 23rd November 2020]

468 China resorting to confrontation along LAC to punish India for rejecting BRI. 3rd July 2020. The Economic Times https://economictimes.indiatimes.com/news/defence/china-resorting-to-confrontation-along-lac-to-punish-india-for-rejecting-bri-swedish-journalist/articleshow/76764152.cms [Accessed 10th December 2020]

469 In 2019 the US goods trade deficit with China amounted to US$345 billion, representing a 17.6% decrease compared with the previous year See: The People's Republic of China: U.S. China Trade Facts. Office of the United States Trade Representative. https://ustr.gov/countries-regions/china-mongolia-taiwan/peoples-republic-china [Accessed 10th December 2020]

470 Waugh, M. The US-China trade war is harming communities in the US. 19th November 2019. VoxEU. https://voxeu.org/article/us-china-trade-war-harming-communities-us [Accessed 10th November 2020].
Tang, F. US trade war has cost China 'almost 2 million industrial jobs'. Investment bank CICC says. 24th July 2019. South China Morning Post. https://www.scmp.com/economy/china-economy/article/3019916/us-trade-war-has-cost-china-almost-2-million-industrial-jobs [Accessed 10th November 2020]

471 Chaziza, M. The Impact of the Coronavirus Pandemic on China's Belt and Road Initiative in the Middle East. 28th April 2020. Middle East Institute https://www.mei.edu/publications/impact-coronavirus-pandemic-chinas-belt-and-road-initiative-middle-east [Accessed 4th December 2020]

472 Lee, YH. Covid 19: the Nail in the Coffin of China's Belt and Road Initiative? 28th September 2020. The Diplomat. https://thediplomat.com/2020/09/covid-19-the-nail-in-the-coffin-of-chinas-belt-and-road-initiative/ [Accessed 4th November 2020]